£3

*Sharing the Desert*

# *Sharing*

The Research Staff of the American West Center

Floyd A. O'Neil, Director

The Tohono O'odham Nation Education Department

Rosilda Manuel, Bernard Siquieros, Directors

# the Desert

## The Tohono O'odham in History

**Winston P. Erickson**

The University of Arizona Press

Tucson & London

The University of Arizona Press
Copyright © 1994
The Tohono O'odham Nation

All rights reserved. Published 1994
Printed in the United States of America
∞ This book is printed on acid-free, archival-quality paper.
99  98  97  96  95  94      6  5  4  3  2  1

Library of Congress Cataloging-in-Publication Data

Erickson, Winston P., 1943–
   Sharing the desert : the Tohono O'odham in history / Winston P.
Erickson, the research staff of the American West Center [and] the
Tohono O'odham Nation Education Department.
     p.  cm.
   Includes index.
   ISBN 0-8165-1490-9 (acid-free paper)
   1. Tohono O'odham Indians—History.  [1. Tohono O'odham
Indians—History.  2. Indians of North America—History.]  I. University
of Utah. American West Center.  II. Tohono O'odham Nation.
Education Dept.  III. Title.                94-12391
E99.P25E75  1994                           CIP
978´.004974—dc                        AC

British Cataloguing-in-Publication Data
A catalogue record for this book is available from the British Library.

# Contents

# *Illustrations*

# *Preface*

This volume is the result of a long-held desire of the Tohono O'odham to have a document-based history. More than a decade ago, the tribe, in association with the American West Center, University of Utah, began a search for historic documents and other sources on which to base such a work. Researchers from the tribe and the center conducted the search at the National Archives and Record Center at Laguna Nigel, California; the National Archives in Washington, D.C.; the Smithsonian Institution; and the Museum of the American Indian in New York.

The libraries of the University of Arizona, Arizona State University, and the Marriott Library, University of Utah, were all very helpful. Dr. Bernard L. Fontana was especially generous in sharing materials that he has collected over many years.

From the tribe, those who assisted in research are Danny Lopez, Kenneth Vasquez, Ambrose Encinas, Bernard Siquieros, Deena Thomas, and Rosilda Manuel. Barbara Emmons of Tucson was helpful in many ways. The gathering effort was financed by a National Endowment for the Humanities grant (ES20719-83).

After the conclusion of the record-gathering stage, curricular items were completed and introduced into the schools on the reservation. Then the tribe's Education Department, headed by Bernard Siquieros, started an effort to create a more comprehensive history of the Tohono O'odham. His efforts, and the efforts of his successor in office,

Rosilda Manuel, were directed toward the production of a volume that would be useful in the schools and would also serve the general reader.

The Arizona Humanities Council funded a portion of the costs of the work, which was a joint project of the Tohono O'odham Nation and the American West Center.

For this stage of the new project, researchers conducted a set of oral history interviews in Tucson, San Xavier, Sells, Ajo, Gila Bend, and Yuma. The O'odham point of view is reinforced by the use of these oral histories. As this work progressed, committees appointed by the tribal government reviewed the work and read the final manuscript aloud to assure its accuracy and sensitivity to O'odham concerns.

The staff of the American West Center, University of Utah, has worked with the tribe for the past fifteen years. Winston P. Erickson was the writer and principal researcher of the book. Others who assisted in various ways are David Hoehner, Colleen Wimmer, and Linda Higgins. June K. Lyman of Phoenix provided grade-leveling assistance and many other favors. Brian Schell, Paul Jager, and Darlene Taylor worked on the maps as credited. Winston P. Erickson did the uncredited maps.

Many cooperative projects are fraught with difficulties. This project was no exception, and this book represents the efforts of the tribe and the American West Center to overcome the inevitable cultural differences to create a history under the parameters set by the tribe. The education officials and the chairmen of the tribe have all been wonderfully dedicated in the completion of the work. Several tribal councils have also contributed willingly, and with criticism that improved the final work.

My part was to serve as researcher, administrator, and coworker with the Tohono O'odham Education Department staff. That was a great pleasure.

Floyd A. O'Neil
*Director*
American West Center
University of Utah

# Introduction

The Tohono O'odham Nation has approximately 17,000 enrolled members, the majority of whom reside on a main reservation of more than 2.5 million acres of southern Arizona land. Three other much smaller reservations include San Xavier near Tucson, Florence near Casa Grande, and Gila Bend, along the Gila River north of the western end of the main reservation.

The Tohono O'odham history text will be used by students at all schools within the Tohono O'odham Nation. Currently, nine schools serve students there, including: Baboquivari Junior/Senior High School, Topawa Middle School, and Sells Primary School, which are administered by the Indian Oasis/Baboquivari Unified School District No. 40; Tohono O'odham High School, Santa Rosa Boarding/Day School, San Simon School, and Santa Rosa Ranch School (grades K-8), which are under the jurisdiction of the Bureau of Indian Affairs, Papago Agency; and the San Xavier Mission School (grades K-8) and Living Word Academy (grades K-12), which are sponsored by religious organizations.

The Tohono O'odham Education Committee/Board of Directors, the Tohono O'odham Legislative Council, and a ten-member history-text committee have carefully reviewed this book. All are in agreement that a book of this nature has been long overdue. It will provide information about the Tohono O'odham that has not previously been available in any one volume, and it will allow members of the Nation to better understand themselves and their government.

The research focused on a useful and somewhat comprehensive history. It provided an opportunity for three Tohono O'odham researchers to become involved in gathering materials from the Museum of the American Indian; the Library of Congress; the National Anthropological Archives; the Smithsonian Institution in Washington, D.C.; the Federal Record Center at Laguna Nigel, California; the University of Arizona Library; the Arizona State University Library; and the Marriott Library, University of Utah. Local resources in Arizona were also used. This was a unique educational experience. Other Tohono O'odham participated in the interview process.

Although this book will be primarily for instruction in the schools, it will also be of interest to other readers. It will educate teachers and community members as well as anyone with an interest in Tohono O'odham history. The reading audience should extend beyond the boundaries of the Tohono O'odham Nation and across the state of Arizona to anyone with concern or curiosity about Native American history.

Sylvester Listo
*Chairman, Tohono O'odham Nation*

Rosilda Lopez Manuel
*Director, Department of Education*

*Sharing the Desert*

# The Land and the O'odham

*At the edge of the world*
*It is growing light.*
*The trees stand shining.*
*I like it. It is growing light.*

*At the edge of the world*
*It is growing light.*
*Up rears the light.*
*Just yonder the day dawns,*
*Spreading over the night.*

    RUTH M. UNDERHILL, *Singing for Power*

From the underworld, I'itoi led our ancestors, the O'odham, upward into their land, a land stark and dry, yet beautiful. With patience, the O'odham came to understand the land, and from it, they learned to shape their lives and their unique and lasting traditions.

Many years ago, the O'odham lands reached as far south as the San Ignacio Arroyo. Perhaps even farther south of this arroyo, the ancient O'odham shared lands with the Seris and some Opatas. The eastern boundary of the traditional O'odham lands was probably the San Miguel River valley north of Cucurpe, but some of the O'odham may have used the area between the San Miguel and the Sonora rivers, and even eastward into the mountains. To the north, not far from the source of the Sonora River, begins the San Pedro River. It flows northward through a valley that borders the eastern boundary of the traditional O'odham lands.

Eventually, the San Pedro River joins the Gila River, which flows west to the Colorado River. The Gila River marks the northern extent of the traditional lands. The Colorado River and the Gulf of California form the western boundary of the lands used by the Tohono O'odham.

These lands encompassed a large portion of what is now called the Sonoran Desert. At various times, the peoples who have come to the

O'odham lands named this area the Pimería Alta and the Papaguería. Now it is the Tohono O'odham Reservation—part of Arizona in the United States and part of Sonora in Mexico. The O'odham shared the border areas of this land with their neighbors, but the central region, from the Altar River to near the Gila River, was exclusively the O'odham homeland.

Wide valleys separated by low mountains are the most common characteristics of this land. The mountain ranges run generally north and south, like most ranges in North America, and they do not extend great distances. They are usually from ten to forty miles in length.

The ranges to the west are the lowest. They rise from broad valleys that have elevations between 300 and 500 feet. The highest point in the Gila Range, the range farthest west, is 3,141 feet. Since many of these mountains do not have a high elevation, their plant and animal life is not much different from the surrounding valleys.

The higher ranges to the east, including the Baboquivari, have forests of desert trees such as palo verde and mesquite. These mountains rise from valley floors of about 3,000 feet to elevations near 7,000 feet. Baboquivari Peak is 7,730 feet high. In the easternmost ranges in the area that is now part of the United States, peaks reach elevations above 9,000 feet. In Sonora, the Sierra Madre Occidental is the easternmost area used by the O'odham. Peaks there exceed 10,000 feet above sea level. These highest ranges have forests of tall pines and vegetation that are very different from the desert in which the O'odham live.

The most prominent points of the Baboquivari Range in central Papaguería are Kitt Peak and the sacred mountain, Baboquivari Peak. I'itoi, the Elder Brother who brought O'odham ancestors to this land, lived in a cave, still obscured by scrub forests and rocky cliffs, on Baboquivari Peak.

Higher mountains with narrower valleys characterize the eastern fringes of O'odham lands, and these more majestic ranges extend much farther north and south. Travelers going east or west may have to cross at high mountain passes rather than go around these mountains. Here the mountains are covered with pinyon and ponderosa pines, and the U.S. government has recognized the value of the forests in these mountains and has designated national forests in several areas.

Scarcity of water defines the desert lands, but there are a few major rivers other than those that form the borders of O'odham lands. They include the Santa Cruz, the Altar, the Magdalena, and the Concepción rivers, and perhaps some of their larger tributaries. But these rivers do not always flow year-round.

Before modern agriculture and cattle raising altered the land and its vegetation, these rivers held more water and did not dry up as quickly during the hot season as they do today. Even then, however, a river such as the Sonoita would surface in specific locations and flow above ground for a few miles, only to sink again into the sand. After a long distance, water would reappear in its channel. Sometimes, under extremely wet conditions, the river would flow above ground all the way to the Gulf of California, but this seldom occurred.

Some streams, which become parched, sandy washes in the dry months, supplement the rivers during the wet season. When a heavy rain saturates the top layer of soil, additional rainwater runs off and eventually collects in washes creating these streams. These intermittent streams then feed the rivers, causing them to flow or even flood for a time.

Before the Spaniards and the Anglo-Americans came to this region, heavy rains often created broad floods of shallow water that moved across the valley floors. Although this kind of flood still occurs, it is much less common than in past years because of changes in the land. These changes are primarily due to erosion caused by more modern land use, especially cattle grazing.

Where the land remains undisturbed, abundant plant life, particularly grasses, acts as an obstacle to moving water. It disperses the water across the valley floor and prevents it from forming streams. However, as the amount of plant life decreases from overgrazing, the water flows faster and has more of a tendency to carve new gullies that will run directly into the washes and riverbeds. The washes then become deeper and wider, and tend to gather larger amounts of water more quickly. This causes more erosion, which widens and deepens the channels even more. Because the deeper washes move the water faster than before, the surface soils have much less water. This poses a serious threat to the survival of some species of plants in the area.

Natural springs in the O'odham lands have given some of the O'odham a reliable water supply. For example, Quitovac in Mexico has a constant supply of water that pours from beneath the edge of a low mesa. Here there is enough water to support a village. Quitobaquito, south of Ajo and just inside what is now the United States, was a village named for small springs. Other small springs are found in the mountains scattered across the O'odham lands.

Because water is scarce and unreliable in most parts of the desert, it was important for O'odham ancestors to find, develop, and use different sources. During part of the year, they gathered rainwater from potholes found in the mountains. These potholes, or *tinajas* as they are sometimes called, are formed when water runs quickly down the slopes of the nearly barren mountains, gathers in the draws, and drops over cliffs, or jumps. Where there are jumps, waterfalls erode the stone to create a basin. The water fills the basin, overflows, then splashes down the slope to the next drop to create another basin. After the rains cease, these catch basins, or tinajas, are full of water, and they serve as natural reservoirs for the animals and some plants of the desert.

Since the ancient O'odham knew where the largest basins were, these potholes became an important water source for them. When evaporation caused by heat and dry air left a lower pothole dry, or the people and animals had consumed all of the water, they climbed higher in the mountains, until all of the basins were empty.

The O'odham had intimate knowledge of the land, and they were able to find other sources of water by digging in washes or other places. The water was brackish or salty at times, but it was enough for survival. This was the situation near the Gulf of California where the Hia C'eḍ O'odham, or Sand People, lived among the dunes.

Two relatively wet seasons mark the climate of this land. The mild winter and the hot summer bring some moisture to the desert. Unlike many areas that have greater rainfall during the colder season, the Sonoran Desert usually receives most of its rainfall during the hot, late-summer months when huge thunderstorms brew above the valleys.

As the rain clouds gather moisture and grow, the winds ease them across the desert valleys toward the mountains. When the peaks disrupt the flow of air, the clouds release torrents of rain on the mountains and nearby valley floors, until the storm's energy dissipates. Depending on the conditions, these rain clouds can come in huge, general storms that sweep in broad bands across a wide area, or they can be small, isolated storms that will flood one village while not a drop falls on a neighboring village a mile or two away.

Thunderstorms here are intense and dangerous, and flooding can occur with little or no warning because floodwaters can travel miles from where the storm occurred. The major danger in storms, however, is the spectacular but deadly lightning, and a fear of lightning is not uncommon in O'odham tradition.

This shrine on the Tohono O'odham Reservation commemorates children who saved the O'odham from a flood. (Courtesy of Venito Garcia Library, Sells)

Summer weather is extreme. Rarely does a gentle rainfall soak the ground over hours or days. Instead, storms crash in, cool the earth, and disperse. But the heat returns quickly, with temperatures up to 120°F. Such extreme heat can last for weeks.

Winter is the season of more gentle rain, but there is usually less precipitation than in late summer. Fortunately for those with a limited water supply, evaporation is not as severe because temperatures are cooler. Temperatures may drop below freezing occasionally, but the cold rarely lasts. Snow seldom falls except on the highest peaks. If the temperature remains much below freezing for more than thirty-six hours, then the saguaro cacti and other plants may suffer damage or even die.

The growing season in O'odham lands is long. In Sells, the normal growing season, determined by the average number of frost-free days, is 264 days. Higher elevations have considerably shorter seasons, and lower areas toward the Gulf of California can farm almost year-round.

Although similar weather patterns prevail throughout O'odham traditional lands, there are some slight variations in climate. To the west are lower and hotter areas that generally receive less rainfall than the east. The higher region between the San Pedro and the Santa Cruz rivers is cooler and receives more rain. These slight climate variations account for differences in the vegetation and in the living conditions of the various groups of O'odham.

Despite the scarcity of water, the Sonoran Desert is reputed to have more species of native plant life than any other of the world's deserts. The diversity of vegetation certainly adds to the beauty and interest of the landscape, particularly for those who visit from different climates. Many travelers are pleasantly surprised by what may be the world's greenest desert: plants in the Sonoran Desert have adapted in such a way that they maintain an intensity of color seldom found in other deserts.

Large stands of trees—palo verde, ironwood (or *palo fierro*), and mesquite—create patches of green in the desert, and the ancient O'od-ham depended on them. Some made hand tools and arrow points from the hard wood of the ironwood tree. Others ground the long mesquite seedpods and palo verde seeds into meal. The trees, compet-ing for water, anchored the banks of washes and arroyos. Mesquite roots can grow sixty feet deep, with more wood below ground than above. These desert trees also have small leaves so that less water evaporates from their surfaces.

Many other desert plants have adapted to the hot, dry climate. Cacti grow hard outer shells to protect their pulpy cores where they store water. Even their prickly needles have a special purpose. The white needles of the cholla not only protect it from the attack of large insects but also reflect the scorching sunlight. Some three hundred species of cactus are native to O'odham lands, ranging in size from small peyote buttons to the sixty-foot-high cardón cactus of Mexico. All have adapted to survive the desert aridity and heat.

Large, broadleaf trees are found only along washes and in other places where water is more plentiful. These riparian species, such as cottonwoods, sycamores, and desert willows, probably have the larg-est leaves of all the plants found in this desert.

Many bushes and shrubs also grace the landscape with greenery. Creosote bushes are common in most of the broad valleys, spacing themselves and often running roots far from the stalks in order to gather as much water as possible from the rains. Ocotillo plants shoot their narrow branches into the air, sprout tiny green leaves during the wet seasons, produce vibrant crimson blossoms, and drop their leaves in dry periods. In some areas, sagebrush prevails, as it does in much of the West. Cholla trees and Bigelow's cholla, because of their many needles, can make life miserable for anyone who accidentally brushes against them.

Grasses, including galleta grass, which can sustain itself even in the sandy soils of O'odham lands to the west, cover the desert floor and provide food for various animals. Many other species of plants add variety to the vegetation of the O'odham lands.

Animals play an important role in the O'odham homeland. Reptiles roam among trees, over rocks, and through the sand. One might see a blur of black stripes on a tiger whiptail lizard as it races past. Unlike the speedy lizards that can dash away from predators, horned lizards, sometimes called horned toads, move at a more leisurely pace. To protect themselves, they have developed the perfect camouflage. Lying close to the ground, the horned lizards' thornlike projections press against the rocks and soil to eliminate any trace of a shadow, and their dust-gray skin blends perfectly with the sand and rock. Even the sharp-eyed red-tailed hawk has difficulty spotting a horned lizard.

Another slow mover is the desert turtle or tortoise. As a youngster, this reptile has noticeable bright bands of yellow-orange on its back. As it grows older, its shell smooths to dull gray. Tortoises have been known to live for as long as seventy years. Another common reptile in O'odham lands is the yellow, red, and black Gila monster, and there are numerous snakes, including rattlesnakes, king snakes, and blue racers.

The coyote is the main large predator, but also in the desert is the occasional mountain lion or a rare black bear. Because of their nocturnal habits, these animals are seldom seen. Overall, the hot desert region is not conducive to the proliferation of large mammals, and there were never very many.

There are more small mammals in the desert, but most of these are nocturnal, too. Jackrabbits and rats are native to the area, as are ringtailed cats, badgers, and skunks. Mice adapted to the dry, hot climate provide food for the rattlesnakes and other predators. Caves in the mountains are home to bats.

Numerous birds also populate the desert. The most visible of the birds are the vultures. The O'odham lands are in the northern range of the black vulture, which shares the sky with the more common turkey vulture and an occasional white-headed caracara. Crows are common and aid in the disposal of carrion. Ravens live in the higher mountains.

The night sky is controlled by owls. Smaller species like the burrowing owl and elf owl are the most common, but there are also desert horned owls. Large predatory birds include buteos like the red-tailed hawk, Harris's hawk, and, infrequently, a golden eagle.

Many smaller birds live in the desert. The cactus wren earned its name by nesting in the tangled branches of the prickly cholla. Sparrows are common, as are Gambel's quail and hummingbirds. Hummingbirds are indispensable to desert plants since they pollinate the flowers while seeking life-sustaining nectar.

Fish did not play much of a role in the O'odham lands. Few rivers were permanent or large enough to sustain fish of edible size. However, the Hia C'eḍ O'odham sometimes harvested fish trapped in the tidal pools in the Gulf of California.


Into these lands, the O'odham emerged. Here their ancestors developed the knowledge, customs, and crafts necessary for survival. They became a kind, gentle, sharing people, and in small groups of extended families, they developed a peaceful way of life, adapting themselves to the dry climate and the diet that the land afforded them.

O'odham traditions helped them survive in the starkly beautiful but far from bountiful land. Except in the few regions where there was continuously flowing water in rivers or springs, living in one place all year was impractical if not impossible. Those who lived along the rivers were able to build more permanent homes, but most O'odham migrated between summer and winter homes where they built brush or mud houses for shelter.

Summer homes were usually made in the valley or at the base of the mountains in what were called field villages, where the O'odham cultivated the alluvial fans, formed when mountain washes flow out onto the flatlands. The water rushing out of the mountains carries mud, sand, and rocks, and as the water slows, the material, called alluvium, settles in a fan-shaped formation at the mountain base.

During the wet season in late July, August, and early September, thunderstorms bring rain, and the traditional O'odham directed the water coming from the mountains so that it would spread across the broad fields. Too much or too little water could be a problem, so agri-

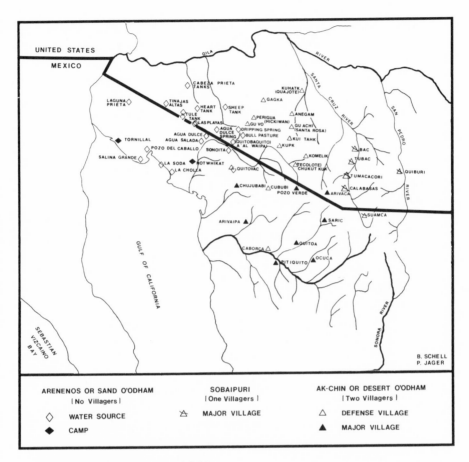

## O'odham groups, pre-1800

culture under such conditions was always fragile. Too much water would wash away the seeds or plants; too little water prevented plowing and stunted plant growth.

The basic native plants used by the O'odham and other peoples of the southern deserts were maize, squash or pumpkins, and beans. If enough rain fell, and if it came early enough, there would be plenty of time for crops to mature before freezing temperatures destroyed them. But if the rains came late in the season, the plants might not mature in time to harvest before the frosts.

Some O'odham cultivated fields farther out in the valley floor, where they diverted washes and even used dikes to build catch basins,

9

called *charcos,* to store water. For the most part, water supplies were not consistent enough for the O'odham to develop permanent canal and irrigation systems like those of the Pimas in the north. However, some of the Sobaipuris may have copied the Pimas where conditions allowed.

When winter approached, the O'odham moved to the mountains, where there were wells, springs, or pools of water in natural catch basins. They called these areas the well villages. Although the need for water was the main reason the O'odham moved to the mountains, hunting was a major source of food and another important reason to travel there for the winter months.

Some of the O'odham—the Hia C'eḍ O'odham of the western region—did not plant crops except in one or two areas because very few places had enough water to support any kind of agriculture. Consequently, the Hia C'eḍ O'odham did not establish summer and winter homes but had to move more often to find enough food and water to sustain themselves.

Even though most of the O'odham cultivated crops, gathering food was nearly a full-time activity. For those who knew how to gather and prepare edible plants and animals, the desert could provide enough food for survival.

One particularly important plant was the saguaro cactus, whose fruit pods were harvested to make wine for the rain-making ceremonies. The O'odham also made preserves of the fruit for later use.

Another staple food in the O'odham diet was the bean pods of mesquite trees. The seeds were too hard to use, but the O'odham either ground the pods into flour or chewed the pod whole. They also ground amaranth seeds into a gruel and ate the leaves of young plants.

The O'odham used even the spiny cholla cactus, drying the buds for later use. When food was scarce, they soaked the buds in water to soften them for eating. Harvested crops also were dried to preserve them until spring and early summer when less food was available, but wild plants constituted a greater portion of the O'odham diet than domestic crops.

O'odham women were traditionally in charge of food preparation and storage. Everyone participated in some gathering, but women gathered most of the food and spent much of their time grinding on *metates*—flat stones on which dry food was crushed so that it could be cooked into a gruel. Much of the food was preserved by drying it in the sun and storing it in large pottery containers called *ollas,* which sometimes were buried underground for safekeeping.

O'odham women also were responsible for carrying water to the village every morning. The older girls often would run several miles to get enough water for drinking, cooking, and cleaning. If a family lacked older girls, the wife would assume the responsibility.

Women also helped during planting and harvesting, but the men did most of the tilling and hoeing, and they also were responsible for hunting. The more experienced men hunted larger game, primarily mule deer and desert bighorn sheep. The young men and boys hunted rabbits and other small animals.

Another important role filled mostly by men was that of the medicine man. When illness became a problem, the O'odham called upon medicine men, the healers who possessed the gifts and knowledge of rituals.

Men also ensured that the group did what needed to be done each day, and they met in the evenings to plan the next day's activities and make decisions about important matters like farming, hunting, defense, and moving. Groups were communal. The elders of the village assembled to make decisions for the whole group.

Although the O'odham traded for some goods, they made almost everything they used. Women made most of the baskets and ollas and other implements of pottery, often working beneath sunshades called *ramadas*. Brush shelters were built easily from local materials, so the O'odham did not have to take them when they moved. The shelters protected them from wind, rain, and sun, but they also allowed air to circulate, which helped keep them cooler in hot summer months. Grass mats, made to sleep on, could be pushed tightly against the walls to keep small animals out.

Because most villages were made up of members of an extended family, and close relatives were not allowed to marry, marriages had to be arranged with people from other villages. Marriages were arranged by parents, or older siblings if the parents were dead. The wife usually left home to move into her husband's house, where she helped her mother-in-law with the domestic chores. The rules were flexible, however, and if the wife's family needed help, the husband could move in with her family instead.

Polygamy was allowed, and some men had two or more wives. If one of the partners in a marriage became unhappy, he or she could leave and return to the original family. Thereafter, family members could arrange another marriage. A woman did not always have a great deal to say about a marriage, but if the union proved to be less than satisfying, she could leave.

Children grew up surrounded by siblings and cousins, free to play until they were about six years old. Often the instructional part of a child's upbringing rested with grandparents and older children because the parents were occupied constantly with food gathering and preparation or other necessities. After the age of six, children began working with older children and adult members of their sex to learn the skills of survival and the traditions of the community.

One of the most noted traditions and important aspects of O'odham society was sharing. The O'odham shared food not only with family members but also with other villages. Most often when a hunter killed a large animal, all the members of the village would partake in the feast. This sharing of goods and food then created a debt that was expected to be repaid whenever the others had a surplus. Those who only took and never gave could eventually become excluded or ignored.

The tradition of sharing united the community and fostered the concept that survival was not just an individual concern. Instead, survival concerned all of the people within a family, a village, or even a region, and sharing extended to cooperation within and between the villages. When one family or village helped another, they did so knowing that when they needed help, they would receive it from their neighbors.

However, loyalty was bound more closely to local groups than to the region because even though the O'odham were unified by similar traditions and language, there were considerable differences among the separate groups. The ancient O'odham had no tribal government and apparently no formal leadership positions beyond those in the village.

Members of neighboring villages often would come together to participate in races and other competitive activities, and gambling was common. These activities were social as well as recreational, providing members of different villages a chance to meet prospective marriage partners. Of course, trading of goods and gossip was also part of the gathering.

Another reason groups might gather and submit to more formal leadership was to defend themselves against a common enemy. The

Apaches are believed to have migrated into the area of O'odham lands in the fifteenth and sixteenth centuries, and they became so despised for their raids that the O'odham word for "enemy" also means "Apache." When the Apaches began to invade O'odham lands, the peaceful O'odham had to gather in larger village groups to defend themselves. At times, the O'odham also assembled to attack the Apaches to prevent future raids.

The Apaches were not interested in much of the land, but they wanted food, goods, women, and children. If warned in time, the O'odham would mobilize to defend against the attacks. After a raid, they would assemble a band of warriors to chase and try to retrieve the captives and possessions the Apaches had taken. For this purpose, someone had to organize the war party and set it in motion, but such leadership and alliances were only temporary.

In fact, the O'odham were not a unified people. Although divided according to dialect within the Uto-Aztecan–derived language of the O'odham, not all of the linguistically related peoples were considered Tohono O'odham. The Pimas of the Gila River spoke a similar, mutually understandable language, but the O'odham did not consider them part of the same family. They were more like distant cousins.

In addition to language divisions, different groups of O'odham also had their own origin legends. Other characteristics used to determine who belonged to which group were physical appearance, behavior, and personality, but the easiest way to tell to which group someone belonged to was to find out where he or she lived.

The Sobaipuris occupied the northeastern lands in the valleys of the Santa Cruz and the San Pedro rivers, and the area in between. They developed traditions of more stable residence than most of the other O'odham and were similar in some ways to the Gila River Pimas. Because their lands were higher, cooler, and had fairly reliable sources of water, many Sobaipuris lived in one place all year except when they were hunting or gathering. The water and good fields also attracted the attention of and were coveted by intruders. Thus the Sobaipuris were to suffer more than the others, and were the first to lose most of their lands as different peoples moved onto the traditional O'odham lands.

However, the first to come into contact with the European invaders were the Himuris. They lived south of the Sobaipuris in a region that extended from the confluence of the Magdalena and Altar rivers to

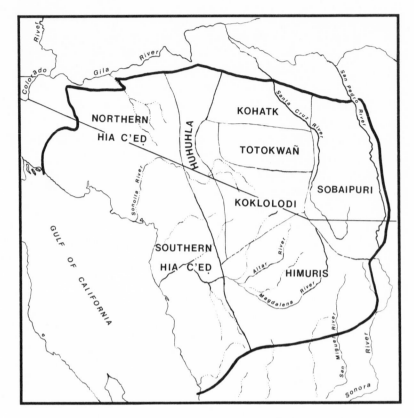

**Tohono O'odham dialect groups, ca. 1700**

the eastern extent of the O'odham lands. This southernmost group of O'odham lived as far north as the present-day city of Nogales on the border between the United States and Mexico.

In the western lands lived the Hia C'eḍ O'odham, who were divided into two major groups, the northern and southern. The southern group shared land with the Seris and may have had more cultural similarities to them than to other O'odham, at least in the far south. The northern group had contact with the Yumas and shared some of their traits.

The Hia C'eḍ O'odham were probably the most linguistically different of the O'odham. They spoke faster than the other groups, but the dialects were still mutually understandable for the most part, although each dialect had exclusive terms not shared with others.

Because the land they inhabited was the driest and hottest of O'odham lands, and had only one or two places suitable for farming, it could not support many people. Nearly all of the Hia C'eḍ O'odham lived as hunter-gatherers, and they used a larger area to sustain themselves than other O'odham. One or two families traveled together in the dry, mostly barren land, much of which consisted of sand dunes stretching to the Gulf of California.

The Hu:huhla group lived east of the Hia C'eḍ O'odham. Their territory extended from the northern border of the Himuris area to just south of the Gila River. The rest of the O'odham considered the Hu:huhla to be the oldest inhabitants of the land. Their land was almost as poor as that of the Hia C'eḍ O'odham, and they were called "orphans" by other groups. Perhaps they had been in the land before I'itoi led the others from the underworld, and the others did not know what to think of them.

South of the lands controlled by the Pimas along the Gila River, and east of the Hu:huhla territory, lived the Kohatk group. The Kohatk were related closely to the Pimas because of considerable trade and intermarriage. Their influence extended as far south as the line between modern Santa Rosa and Tucson.

The central area of the O'odham lands is around Ge Aji, and a group of O'odham called the Totokwan built and inhabited the villages there. This may have been the ceremonial center of the O'odham, or at least of the northern groups.

The other linguistic group is the Koklolodi, which occupied territory between the Totokwan and the Himuris, and the Hu:huhla and the Sobaipuris.

These divisions within the O'odham are somewhat a matter of opinion. Different investigators have found more or fewer groups, and defined different borders for the various groups. One explanation for various historical interpretations is that differences between groups were constantly blurred by contact between neighboring peoples.

One group of O'odham, the Sobas (probably a subgroup of the Himuris), lived in the southeastern O'odham lands along the Altar River. They were the first to interact with the Spanish missionaries, and thus were the earliest victims of Spanish encroachment. They either died or joined with other groups as they lost their lands to the Spaniards and suffered from Apache raids.

There is some debate regarding the Hohokam (or Huhugam) people who created the buildings that have become the ruins of Casa

Grande and who lived in other parts of the Papaguería. Although some people assume that the Hohokam were ancestors of the O'odham, others argue that the archaeological evidence does not support that theory.

The ancestors of today's Tohono O'odham were a peaceful, nonaggressive people who usually were able to reside amiably with their neighbors. Most of the neighbors were also peaceful. However, some tribes, such as the Apaches, dominated the less-aggressive peoples of the region.

The Seris, the O'odham's neighbors to the south, inhabited the lands south of the San Ignacio River. Many of them lived on the coast and sought some of their food from the sea. They were nomadic or seminomadic, but there is no indication that they were hostile to the O'odham before Spaniards began using warriors from one tribe to force Spanish will on the others.

To the east of the Seris were the Lower Pimas and the Opatas. The linguistically related Lower Pimas occupied the lower San Miguel River area but probably had little contact with the O'odham except for trading. The Opatas lived near the headwaters of the San Miguel and Sonora rivers, and maybe as far north as the source of the San Pedro River. The Opatas may have been expanding their territory, and through the years, they may have been involved in separating the Lower and Upper Pima groups. Conflicts between the O'odham and these other tribes involved land use rather than raiding for plunder and subsistence.

North of the Opatas and east of the O'odham lands were the Sumas, Jocomes, and the Apaches. The Sumas were Uto-Aztecan but may have merged with the intruding Athapascans, linguistically related groups of Indians who first were identified in the far north and then migrated southward. Included in the Athapascans are the Apaches and Navajos. Both tribes were very different from most of the Indian groups in what is now the southwestern United States and the northwestern states of Mexico. These hunter-gatherers and aggressive warriors probably began moving into the area shortly before the Spaniards began their missionary activities in that region during the late sixteenth century.

Along the Gila River to the north lived the O'odham's Pima cousins. They were very closely related, not only linguistically but also economically and socially. Much trading, sharing, and intermarriage occurred between these Pimas and the northern bands of the O'od-

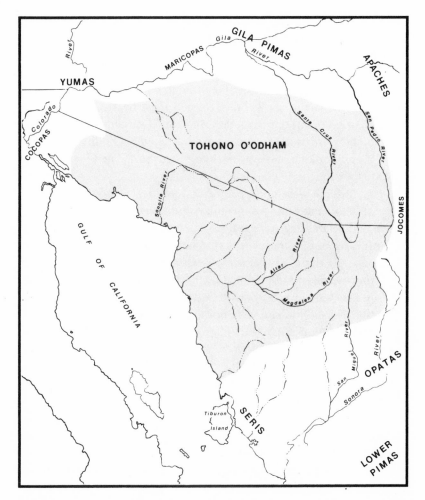

**Papaguería and neighbors of the Tohono O'odham, ca. 1700**

ham. The Gila River Pimas were distinguished by permanent houses and their large fields with extensive irrigation canals, and they were wealthy compared to the Tohono O'odham. In times of food shortages, the Pimas helped the people from the desert, and they also helped fight off the invaders.

Westward along the Gila River were the Cocopas and the Yuma Indians. The Yumas lived along the Colorado River and shared hunting grounds with the few Hia C'ed O'odham of the area. They were trading partners and occasionally squabbled over land use or occupancy.

The Hia C'eḍ O'odham would sing for the Yumas in exchange for food, and they also traded baskets and shells.

Many of these neighbors provided trading partners for the O'odham. The Tohono O'odham had knowledge of tribes as far away as the Hopi and Zuni, with whom they traded the fruit, syrup, and seeds of the saguaro cactus, cholla buds, roasted agave hearts, sleeping mats, baskets, dried meat, animal hides, and salt. Occasionally songs and ceremonies were traded, too. In exchange, the O'odham received corn, beans, cooking implements, and other tools. The O'odham also traded labor for food and goods.

The O'odham were not a people in a political sense. Instead, their sense of belonging came from similar traditions and ways of life, language and related legends, and experiences shared in surviving in a beautiful but not entirely hospitable land. They learned to work together and to share all of their possessions. Because they kept only what they needed to use every day, they did not accumulate worldly possessions, which were a burden and a luxury they could not afford.

Although the O'odham were not unified by any form of tribal government or religious organization, groups of extended families planted, harvested, hunted, and moved to their gathering fields together. Groups also would assemble to defend themselves against aggressors.

Other Native American peoples in the region were not attracted to most of the O'odham lands because the living conditions were so harsh. The O'odham did not wish to go elsewhere, but although they did not develop aggressive, warlike characteristics, they did develop defensive skills to protect themselves from attackers. When threatened from the outside, the O'odham joined together in large groups and prepared for war. Then the O'odham men became fierce warriors. For the most part, however, the O'odham preferred to remain to themselves in peace and quiet. They would rather meet with other people for friendly competition or to trade their wares.

The O'odham made this region their home. They established their traditions and used those traditions as the framework for their lives and beliefs. They knew the desert. They knew the plants and animals. And with that knowledge, they survived as a peaceful, singing people.

# 2

## Tranquility Disturbed

*This season is very dangerous to man, and far too often the injurious*
*effects of the burning sun are apparent, especially to foreigners. When*
*such people, whose bodies are not yet accustomed to this penetrating*
*heat, walk for long in the sun or, more often, stand still somewhere for*
*a time, the rays, they say in Sonora, have a way of pressing down*
*upon the body.*

IGNAZ PFEFFERKORN, *Sonora: A Description of the Province*

The earliest written sources of the history of the Tohono O'odham correspond to the time when the influence of exotic cultures and intrusions by different peoples began to exert pressure on the O'odham society. Most of the specific information about early O'odham history comes from records kept by Europeans who moved into O'odham lands as missionaries or as Spanish military personnel. Apparently, during the latter part of the seventeenth century, changes began to come to the O'odham lands.

Although we do not know exactly when the Apaches moved into the Sonoran Desert, evidence points to the fifteenth century. These migrants from the north had little interest in cultivating the stubborn desert soils, but the Apaches knew that if they attacked a more settled people, they could replenish their supplies and gain commodities for trade. Thus, the many peoples of this area—the Pima, the Opatas, the O'odham, and others—feared the Apaches and considered them a formidable enemy.

Because the Apaches invaded from the northeast, the O'odham in the eastern regions suffered the most from their raids. Although the O'odham were attacked throughout the Altar and Magdalena river valleys, the Sobaipuri groups were raided the most often.

The traditional land of the Sobaipuris between the San Pedro and the Santa Cruz rivers is mountainous and forested. Along the rivers, they built stable dwellings and some well-developed irrigation systems. The permanent water supplies enabled them to live in the villages year-round and store all of their food in one place. When the

Apaches moved in, these developments became a disadvantage for the Sobaipuris. Their villages seemed to fit the Apaches' needs better than the broad desert valleys to the west, and the Apaches not only raided the Sobaipuris for food, but often occupied their village sites.

In the sixteenth century, other groups from the distant European continent began to enter O'odham lands. The O'odham were not aware that Columbus and his successors had discovered the Western Hemisphere, nor did they know about the conquest of Mexico by Cortés. However, these events eventually held grave consequences for them, and they certainly heard rumors about these new people long before any arrived in O'odham lands.

The European explorers moved into lands that native peoples had inhabited for many years. Driven by tales of wealth, these intruders searched for treasures that could be shipped back to Europe. They hoped to make themselves wealthy men and to increase the size and wealth of the empire they were building. They did not respect the Indians' rights but instead claimed all of the land for their king, who, in turn, appointed rulers and church leaders to govern it.

In 1528, Pánfilo de Narváez landed in what is now Florida with six hundred colonists, all hoping to find the fabled province of Apalachen. They were disappointed to encounter only a few humble villages of the native people. After disease and warfare destroyed most of Narváez's forces, the rest retreated to the coast. Here Narváez and his men built horsehide boats to carry them to the Spanish colonies in what is now Mexico. When they passed the mouth of what we now call the Mississippi River, a storm wrecked all the boats, and the group was stranded on the coast. Narváez died in the accident.

Most of the survivors eventually died from starvation, disease, exposure, or attacks by the native people. Some were captured and spent nearly six years as slaves. Eventually, Alvaro Núñez Cabeza de Vaca escaped with three others. Among them was Esteban the Moor.

After their escape, de Vaca and his companions traveled west to avoid the hostile Indians who had enslaved them. Eventually they crossed the eastern end of the Sonoran Desert as they headed south to New Spain. The account of their visit is the first record of Europeans in O'odham lands. It marks the beginning of the monumental changes that Europeans would bring to this land in the coming centuries.

Not long after his first visit, Esteban the Moor returned as a guide for a Franciscan missionary, Fray Marcos, whom the Spanish government had commissioned to find the Seven Cities of Cíbola. Stories circulating among the colonists said these cities held vast amounts of wealth. Because of these rumors, Fray Marcos went north to investigate the truth.

We can be fairly certain that Esteban passed through Sobaipuri lands, and he eventually reached the Zuni pueblos that lay north of their land. The Zunis killed him because he violated sacred Zuni practices. Fray Marcos had lingered behind Esteban and probably traveled no farther than the area of the Gila River Pimas. When he learned of Esteban's death, he decided to return to New Spain to report his discoveries. Like many before him, he said the cities of Cíbola were more impressive than the city of Mexico. This report led to the renowned Coronado expedition.

In 1540, the Coronado expedition traveled through the eastern edge of O'odham lands. When the expedition finally reached its destination, the men were disappointed to find only the impoverished Zuni pueblos. However, this event was particularly important for the O'odham because it was their first exposure to the power of Europeans; more than a hundred armed men with horses traveled through O'odham lands.

By the end of 1540, European adventurers had explored the eastern, southern, and western borders of O'odham land. The explorers confirmed that California was a peninsula, and therefore the Gulf of California would not supply a northwest passage. About that time, a ship that was to support Coronado's expedition carried men up the Colorado River beyond its confluence with the Gila River. One of Coronado's lieutenants, Melchor Díaz, who had planned to meet these men but unfortunately missed them, led a group of Spaniards across O'odham land from San Geronimo to the Colorado River.

Because these explorers discovered no great wealth there, the Spaniards left O'odham lands almost untouched for more than a century. They did, however, leave reminders of their presence. Metal tools, such as knives and cooking utensils, were interesting and useful, but the food that the Europeans brought with them was perhaps more important.

Many native peoples of the Sonoran Desert adopted wheat, just as the Europeans adopted maize. Because wheat could be planted in early winter and harvested in the spring (if enough water were available), many peoples, including the O'odham, could have two harvests a year. By trading with neighboring tribes to the south, the O'odham acquired European metal tools and the seed for growing wheat.

## Spanish intrusions on O'odham lands

**Legend**

◇ WATER WELL
▲ INDIAN VILLAGE
○ SPANISH PRESIDIO
● SPANISH REAL (ARMY CAMP)
▨ FATHER KINO'S PIMERIA ALTA
□ KINO CHURCH
▦ GILA TRAIL
▦ CAMINO DEL DIABLO
● MODERN CITY

(Based on a map by B. Schell)

UNITED STATES
MEXICO

GILA RIVER

PHOENIX ●
GILA BEND
TULE TANK
YUMA ●
PUERTO PEÑASCO

SAN ANDRES
ENCARNACION
SAN FERNANDO ▲
SAN GREGORIO ▲
MONTEZUMA'S TANK ◇
SANTA CATALINA
LA VICTORIA DE OJIO
SAN CLEMENTE
EL VALLE
SAN EUGENIO
SAN PANTALEON (ARIBABIA) ▲
JIASPE ▲
SAN SALVADOR ▲
LOS ALAMOS ▲
SANTA CRUZ DE GUYBANIPITEA
QUIBURI ○
SAN REYES
LOS REYES
SAN JOAQUIN
SANTA MARIA
LAS NUTRIAS
TERRENATE
CANANEA
GAUCHI ▲
CORODEGAUCHI ●
FRONTERAS ●
NACOSARI ○
ARIZPE ●
DOLORES □
BACANUCHE □
REMEDIOS □
MAGDALENA □
SAN IGNACIO □
IMURIS □
COCOSPORA □
SAN LAZARO □
BACOANCOS □
SANTA ANA
SANTA TERESA
TUBATAMA
BUSANIC □
TUCABAVIA □
SANTA GERTRUDIS DEL SARIC □
OQUITOA
PITIQUIN
CABORCA □
VALENTIN □
ALTAR ○
VACRIA ▲
BACAPA ▲
SAN RAFAEL ▲
AGUA SALADA ◇
SANTA BRIGIDA ▲
SAN MARCEL (SONOITA) ▲
SAN SERGUIO (QUITOBAQUITO) ▲
EL GAGA (KAKA) ▲
AJO ●
SAN BONIFACIO (OAJOTE) ▲
VOTUM (COCKLEBURI) ▲
ANAGAM (ANEGAM) ▲
ADIDA ▲
BATKI (VAT-JEKI) ▲
SAN SERAFIN (AKCHIN) ▲
TUBAC □
GUEVAVI
SAN CAYETANO DEL TUMACACORI
SAN XAVIER DEL BAC ▲
SAN COSME ▲
TUCSON ▲
SAN AGUSTIN ▲

GULF OF CALIFORNIA

SEBASTIAN VIZCAINO BAY

Although some O'odham had seen the Spanish explorers' horses, they did not immediately use these animals for transportation. A stray or captured horse more likely appeared to be a source of food, just like any other large game animal. In fact, the O'odham did not begin to adopt the domestic animals of the Europeans until after the Spaniards had built missions on their lands, more than 150 years later.

After explorers discovered new mines in Sonora, Spanish colonists pushed rapidly northward. The early Spaniards had no desire to colonize places where there was no source of immediate wealth, but where mines were established, they often exploited native peoples by using them like slaves. By 1623, the Spanish military had subdued the Mayo and Yaqui Indians and taken control of their lands, and Spanish settlement had reached the lands of O'odham trading partners.

As mining activity in southern Sonora increased, it attracted settlers who came to cultivate the land. During the growing season, the farmers earned their living by selling food to those working the mines. Between seasons, farmers often supplemented their income by working in the mines themselves.

With mining activity to the south and east of O'odham lands, it is likely that an occasional prospector wandered into O'odham territory, but no records verify this. If prospectors did come into this area, they must not have found any mineral discoveries to attract Spanish settlement. For the most part, the O'odham remained unaffected by the early Spaniards searching for mineral wealth.

In late 1686, however, the leaders of the Jesuit missionary system in New Spain (which is now Mexico) decided to send Father Eusebio Francisco Kino to the northwestern extremes of Spanish settlements. For fifty years, missionaries had been in southern Sonora, laboring to change and convert the native people. The priests were convinced that the Indians would eventually adopt Spanish ideas of civilization, and the Jesuit leaders decided to extend the influence of the Catholic church. They assigned Kino to establish missions in O'odham lands, in what the Spaniards called Upper Pimería.

Priests already were instructing the Opatas and the lower Pimas at missions bordering O'odham lands, and they were able to observe the ways of the O'odham. Because the O'odham cultivated wheat and used European tools, the priests assumed they would also embrace Catholicism and want missions built on their land. Perhaps because the O'odham could see the advantages the Europeans had to offer, such as tools, wheat, and the use of domestic animals, they welcomed the Spanish priests.

Father Kino arrived in the Pimería Alta in March 1687. He built a church and established his headquarters at Cosari on the San Miguel River. For much of the remainder of his life, he taught, preached, and explored in the lands of the O'odham and beyond.

According to Father Kino's records, the O'odham were friendly and enthusiastic toward him and his companions. Kino and his party traveled often and frequently stopped in the rancherías and villages to talk. Father Kino was well liked and had a moderating influence when problems arose between the O'odham and the Spanish military or settlers.

With their acceptance of Father Kino, the Tohono O'odham opened the door for more intensive missionary work by the Jesuit priests. When Kino asked for assistance, more missionaries moved into the region, and it became necessary to establish more churches and farms. The area they chose to settle was along the Altar River, where the O'odham cultivated fields with irrigation canals like those of the Sobaipuris and the Gila River Pimas. Once they had established missions, the priests invited the O'odham to work on the farms, exposing them to both the teachings of Christianity and European methods of farming and of raising cattle and sheep.

The missionaries and Spanish authorities intended to change the traditions of native peoples, and they encouraged the O'odham to accept a European way of life. They wanted the O'odham to build permanent structures for homes, wear clothing that covered most of the body at all times, own private property, and, of course, take part in Christian ceremonies.

For the most part, the O'odham viewed these changes with skepticism. The heat of the desert was not conducive to permanent dwellings, nor to heavy clothes that cover the entire body. Their children ran naked for the first several years of their lives. Men wore breechcloths held by a belt, and women wore only skirts. These clothes could be made of animal hides or cloth woven from plants, such as cotton grown by the O'odham in the few well-watered places or, more likely, grown by the Gila River Pimas, their trading partners to the north.

Perhaps the most foreign concept that the Spaniards introduced to the O'odham was the idea that one man could own property that was protected by legal rights. Tradition told them that families had the right to use the fields, and that a family's ability to cultivate the land determined the size of the field. Families also had rights to gather in areas where certain foods, such as saguaro fruits, were abundant. Because they used what they needed and shared any surplus food they harvested, the O'odham had no need for private property.

The O'odham had no formal laws either. Individuals or families maintained order and proper decorum, and people who went against customs were asked to leave. Those who left either learned to survive alone or joined another group.

To the Spaniards, such loose control seemed uncivilized, and both church and government authorities sought to alter native people's lives. They expected all the Indians to behave like Spanish people, to give up native traditions, and to begin to live under Spanish laws. Although the church and state worked together to bring their sense of order to the newly discovered peoples, the missionaries had the task of "civilizing" the natives of the Americas. Indians who refused to accept Spanish laws and customs usually were punished severely.

The Spaniards believed that severe punishment would set an example for the larger community and show other people the result of improper behavior. They thought punishment would encourage the natives to accept what the Spaniards considered proper behavior. Traditionally, however, the O'odham avoided physical punishment. They showed disapproval of actions by facial expression or ostracism.

The Spanish military was known for being extremely harsh with any who opposed it, and to some extent, the O'odham, as well as other Native Americans, benefited from the presence of the Jesuit fathers, who often acted as mediators between the O'odham and the military. It is likely that the military would have slaughtered many more rebels if the priests had not interceded.

The Spanish military did help the O'odham, too, however. The more peaceful tribes of what is now northern Mexico and the southwestern United States welcomed the Spaniards as allies against the Apaches. The Spanish military, with its horses and organization, had a distinct advantage over the Apaches. Because of this, the O'odham often joined forces with the Spaniards, and in many battles, their ability to fight and defend their lands won the Spaniards' respect.

The Sobas of the Altar Valley and the Sobaipuris were the most skilled O'odham warriors. Because they lived on the borders of O'odham lands, they often had to defend themselves against other people. The Apaches were particularly attracted to those settlements.

The Sobas' and Sobaipuris' permanent homes and irrigation systems with reliable water sources were able to support larger populations and also enabled them to bring together a large number of warriors in a united cause. The Sobaipuris alone may have numbered close to seven thousand at the time of the Spaniards' arrival.

The Spaniards benefited from the skill of allies like the Sobas and the Sobaipuris, but alliances never lasted for long. Spanish forces were constantly confronted with uprisings by native groups. The Apaches may have been constant opponents, but at times the Tarahumaras, the Opatas, the Seris, and the O'odham rose up to defend their rights to the lands occupied by the Spanish invaders. Often the Spaniards had to rush to a troubled spot bolstered by whatever allies they could muster at the time. The Spaniards then maintained tight control until they left to put down a rebellion in another location.

Because the various O'odham groups were not organized under a governing group or one leader, different bands or villages sometimes engaged in power struggles. When Kino first arrived in Cosari in 1687, the people living there were fighting with the Sobas of the Altar Valley, who had killed the leader of the Cosari band. Even within the various bands of the O'odham, there was occasional fighting. To help his missionary efforts, Kino sought to unify or, at the very least, pacify such hostile groups among the O'odham, and he and his companions achieved some peace among southern O'odham by giving gifts of food and other supplies.

The Spanish government also created civilian offices among the natives, issuing canes as symbols of authority. The Spaniards hoped this granting of authority would help establish order among the native people, but the civilian offices represented by the canes probably were not very important to the O'odham. Since the Spaniards usually gave the canes to leaders of the village, it is unlikely the canes increased or changed the power or respect for the newly commissioned leader. Moreover, because the O'odham did not recognize Spanish authority, these canes did not have the same meaning for the O'odham as they did for the Spaniards. The O'odham probably accepted the canes as interesting gifts or curiosities.

By 1694, missions had extended beyond Cosari (or Dolores, as Kino's church was called), to Remedios, San Ignacio, Imuris, Magdalena, and Tubutama. The Spanish missionaries were expanding their religious influence in a relatively friendly fashion, but all was not quiet for the missions and their military compatriots. There were constant problems with the native peoples, and military forces moved continually from one rebellion to another.

In March of 1694, several horse herds were stolen from the missions in Sonora, and the Spaniards suspected the Sobaipuris. The Spanish authorities sent Lieutenant Antonio Solís to investigate in the villages on the San Pedro and Santa Cruz rivers, and at Bac. One day Solís rode into a village without warning and surprised the Indians, who began to run from the soldiers. When Solís discovered a meat-drying frame covered with what he assumed was horse meat, he and his soldiers killed three men and captured two others. Only then did they learn that the meat was venison. The Spaniards left that village and continued on to Bac. When their search finally ended, they had found no evidence to condemn the Sobaipuris.

In spite of this incident, in May 1694, the O'odham joined forces under Solís with the Opatas and the Spaniards to fight against the Apaches. They won the battle by killing many of the opposing warriors and capturing women and children, whom they later sent to work in mines and as house servants in areas to the south. After this victory, Solís became a hero among the Spanish military, and the O'odham gained the reputation of being capable warriors.

When a missionary at Tubutama later complained of discontent among the O'odham, the military sent Solís to solve the problem. Solís and his men captured the two men who instigated the unrest, and although their fate is uncertain, it is known they received punishment. When the military was involved, rebels generally were hanged. Whatever means Solís used to punish the men did seem to silence the unrest at Tubutama, however. Later that year, the O'odham remained allied with the Spanish military to fight the Apaches and Janos invaders in Opata country.

Reports of success from Father Kino, the military commander, and the missionary at Tubutama impressed the Spanish leaders. Deciding that the Pimería was a good location to expand their activity, they assigned two new missionaries to the area. One went to Cocospora, and another, Father Francisco Xavier Saeta, went to Caborca, where he established the Concepción mission.

Although Solís suppressed the trouble at Tubutama, many O'odham resented the leaders' punishment. Adding to the tension was an Opata Indian whom the missionary had hired to be chief herdsman of the mission's sheep and cattle. The Opata exerted undue authority over many of the O'odham who were obliged to work under his supervision, and when the missionary left to observe Holy Week at the end of March 1695, the overseer began beating one of the O'odham.

**27**

The man called his friends for help, and they killed the Opata. The O'odham of Tubutama, releasing pent-up frustration with the Spaniards, killed two other Opatas, destroyed sacred objects, set fire to the church, and slaughtered the cattle.

The rebellion spread down the Altar River to other Spanish settlements, gathering sympathizers along the way. When the rebels reached Caborca, they met with Father Saeta. Even though he had heard of the disturbance, Father Saeta thought the attackers had been Jocomes, and he was completely unaware that he was meeting with the rebels themselves. When he said goodbye, they pulled out their weapons. The rebels then killed Father Saeta and all the mission assistants, and after slaughtering or scattering the animals, they returned home.

The Spaniards organized an army of various Indian tribes, including some O'odham, and marched down the valley, burying the bodies of those killed in the rebellion. The O'odham, knowing they would not be safe from the Spaniards' revenge, left their homes for more remote areas. Tepoca Indians, contrary to instructions from their Spanish leaders not to kill, captured and killed one sick woman. Seris found a man with two boys, and although the man escaped and one of the boys was protected by the Spanish leader of the patrol, the Seris shot the other boy (who was baptized before he died). At Pitquin, the Spaniards captured a woman and two young girls. They interrogated, baptized, and then executed the woman because her village had participated in the rebellion.

As they retreated to bury the remains of the martyred Father Saeta in Cucurpe, the Spaniards turned their horses into the O'odham wheat fields, destroying the food supplies in Caborca and other villages in the Altar Valley. Nevertheless, the Spaniards failed to find those responsible for the murders, and they had lost control of the Altar Valley.

After Indian rebellions, Spanish military forces usually recaptured the land and severely punished the rebels and their supporters. Sometimes they even punished those who remained neutral and did not oppose the rebellion. Kino was aware of this, and he discussed the villagers' fate with General Jironza, the commanding military officer of the northwestern Spanish settlements. They agreed to offer the O'odham who were not involved in the rebellion the chance to help bring the rebels to justice and thereby avoid a military invasion. The peaceful villages agreed to the plan and helped return some of the stolen vestments from the destroyed church buildings of Tubutama. The

O'odham believed Kino's promise that those who helped bring in the guilty would earn peace and a general pardon.

However, the Spanish military and secular authorities were not sure that this would send the O'odham the right message. Some wanted the rebels severely punished as an example of Spanish power and expectations. A large military force led by Solís marched into San Ignacio, and then Tubutama and Oquito, killing some O'odham in surprise attacks.

The O'odham feared more of this kind of treachery when they saw such a large force in their territory. Kino, however, convinced the *alcalde,* or mayor, of El Tupo to bring his people to meet the army outside the village, and to bring the guilty rebels with them. Kino assumed that the guilty would receive just punishment and that peace for the innocent could therefore be maintained.

The Spanish army and about fifty O'odham met at El Tupo on June 9, 1695. After leaving their weapons in a grove of mesquite trees some distance from the meeting place, the O'odham delegation went unarmed into the camp, where they were encircled by Spanish soldiers on horseback. Those guilty of participation in the rebellion were pointed out, but when the Spaniards bound the accused, others became nervous and began to look for escape.

When the governor of Dolores, an O'odham, grabbed one of the rebels by the hair and identified him as one of the murderers, Solís decapitated the man with one stroke of his cutlass. The O'odham then became frightened and tried to break through the line of mounted soldiers, but they were trapped in the circle. In the end, the soldiers and their Tepoca Indian allies killed forty-eight O'odham. This incident became known as *La Matanza,* The Slaughter.

Of those killed, probably only eighteen were guilty of rebellion and involved in the slaying of Father Saeta. Kino felt that the other thirty were innocent people who had been trying to prevent more bloodshed and antagonism. Among those killed in this disaster were the alcalde of El Tupo, who had recently become governor because of his efforts to secure peace, and the captain of El Bosna, who had rendered valuable assistance to the Spaniards. This type of action often occurred in the Americas when Europeans attempted to control the native populations, and the Spaniards frequently relied on brute force and fear as weapons against the O'odham, resulting in bitterness and prolonged enmity.

After the slaughter, the Spaniards thought the O'odham were completely intimidated, and the army withdrew to confront the Apaches and other tribes to the east and north. The army left only a few soldiers to guard the missions.

As soon as the army was gone, many relatives and sympathizers of those killed at El Tupo attacked and burned the missions at Tubutama and Caborca. Then, with three hundred warriors, they moved toward Imuris and San Ignacio. Father Campos, who was in charge of those missions, was warned of the impending attack and escaped, but the O'odham rebels destroyed the buildings at Imuris, San Ignacio, and Magdalena. The rebels killed no one in these attacks.

The Spaniards promptly assembled an army that included about 150 Spanish soldiers and more than 100 allied native warriors. Among them were 42 O'odham who had remained loyal to the Spaniards.

Although the O'odham at Tubutama offered to engage in peace talks, Spanish forces attacked the mission at night and then destroyed the fields and provisions they found between Tubutama and Saric.

On August 6, 1695, some of the O'odham, including the chief of Tucubavia, visited the general of the Spanish forces to begin negotiations to end hostilities in the north. Once again, O'odham leaders promised to surrender those who led the insurrection as the price for peace. However, the Spaniards were not ready for peace until all areas of the rebellion were subdued, and the general turned his attention to Caborca, where the natives were distrustful of the Spaniards because of the slaughter at El Tupo.

Then Kino took control of the negotiations with the O'odham. Against Kino's wishes, the army supplied an escort of natives to travel with him to Caborca. When they arrived, the army captured women and children and killed two O'odham. Later, the military realized the Caborcans had nothing to do with killing Saeta, nor did any of the other villages in that area, and they blamed the men from Tubutama and Oquitoa.

The army returned to the main camp, continued negotiations, and arranged a treaty with the O'odham requiring their leaders to seek out and deliver those involved in the uprising, and those who aided in the murder of Saeta. The O'odham leaders also had to invite the Jesuit fathers back to newly restored missions. According to the Spanish account, the negotiations ended in peace, with mutual trust and friendship reestablished. The O'odham must have felt differently.

Within the vast area of the Pimería at the time of the rebellion, the Spaniards occupied only the Altar River valley and the area around the Magdalena River and its tributaries. With perennial rivers that flowed year-round, these areas were much more conducive to European farming than those to the north.

Before 1696, the O'odham in the north remained undisturbed and lived as they had before, except for a few visitors such as Father Kino and his companions. They had begun trading for European tools and using some agricultural products such as wheat, but otherwise, the O'odham had not been greatly affected by Spanish culture. The Hia C'ed O'odham to the west remained particularly isolated from Spanish influence because their arid region was unattractive for farming and extensive exploration.

In 1696, Kino traveled to Mexico City to request more missionaries for the Pimería. When he arrived, his superiors reassigned him to missions in California, but when supply problems forced those missions to close, he received instructions to return to the Pimería to establish missions among the Sobaipuris. The Spaniards also assigned five more missionaries, expanding their contact with the O'odham in the north.

Earlier in his travels, Kino had visited the upper San Pedro River settlements, where he had become acquainted with Chief Coro, the most influential leader of the Sobaipuris in that area. Coro was known for his success against the Apaches, and he often allied himself with the Spanish military to fight them. Coro's band at Quiburi was the largest on the San Pedro.

Downriver, to the north, other Sobaipuris lived under the leadership of Coro's main rival, Humari, whose main village was called Ojio. Kino had met Humari when Humari made a trip to Dolores, where he and his two sons were baptized.

In 1697, when a large party of Spaniards explored the San Pedro River valley, Kino used his influence with these Sobaipuri leaders to establish missions there. At the same time, the military officer issued canes of office to the leaders of the villages in an effort to develop a civil order that the Spaniards could understand.

Kino and others on the trip indicated in their diaries that more than fifteen villages, with more than two thousand people, existed along the San Pedro River. The diaries describe how the O'odham developed irrigation canals to water fields where they grew crops such as calabashes, beans, and corn, as well as cotton for clothing. Unfortunately, these eastern O'odham did not survive long under the pressures exerted by the Apaches. Even with the help of Spanish forces, the O'odham could not prevent the Apaches from taking the area, and to make matters worse, the two Sobaipuri factions often fought among themselves.

After Kino's expedition to the Sobaipuris, Chief Coro became famous for fighting the Apaches. Almost three hundred Apaches attacked a village near Coro's Quiburi, killing a number of the Sobaipuris and driving many others away from the village. However, as the Apaches settled down to enjoy the spoils of their victory, to roast and dry the meat from the slaughtered horses and cows, Coro arrived. He brought with him not only his own warriors, but others who had been in Quiburi to trade.

When the Apache chief saw that the odds were not in his favor, he suggested that they determine the outcome of the conflict with a man-to-man fight rather than a general battle. Coro agreed, and each leader chose ten of his best warriors. The Apache and Sobaipuri men were skilled with their bows and arrows, but the O'odham warriors were much better at parrying the arrows with their shields. Near the end of the fight, Coro entered the battle. He fought the Apache chief, knocked him to the ground, and bashed his head with a rock. The Apaches watching the contest realized they were losing the battle, which meant they would quickly become captives. They bolted for freedom, but the Sobaipuris gave chase and killed many of them.

Word of the victory filtered south to the Spanish authorities, who found it difficult to believe the magnitude of the battle. They dispatched envoys to verify the claims, and when the envoys arrived, they found the battleground strewn with victims, as many as the stories had claimed. In the eyes of the Spaniards, this event cemented Coro's reputation as a great leader against the Apaches.

But Coro knew his conflicts with the Apaches were far from over. Shortly after his victory, he moved his entire village to Los Reyes on a tributary of the Santa Cruz River. Although Coro later moved his band back to the San Pedro, they did not remain there, marking the beginning of the Sobaipuris' permanent retreat from the San Pedro River drainage.

In January 1697, Kino drove cattle into the Santa Cruz Valley to begin a ranch at Bac. This was the beginning of the San Xavier del Bac mission, which later became the first reservation for the O'odham within the United States. At that time, however, it was simply a cattle ranch, and it was quite a few years before missionaries made it their official residence.

Mission San Xavier del Bac, "The White Dove of the Desert" (Courtesy of Special Collections, University of Arizona Library)

After the expedition to the San Pedro River villages, Kino began exploring the rest of the Papaguería. He was mainly interested in the Indians to the north along the Gila River, and to the west near California. Apparently, Kino did not know that more than a hundred years earlier, Spaniards had explored the Gulf of California and the lower section of the Colorado River. His early maps portray California as an island. Kino was particularly interested in California because of his early missionary activity there, which had been terminated due to supply problems. He therefore continued to search for a way to California from his Sonora location, and in the process, he crossed O'odham lands using many different routes.

Reports from Kino and his companions tell how they came upon large numbers of O'odham in villages. The native people assembled along the way to see the white man in the black robe, and the animals that carried him and members of his party. The priests and their guards mistook the O'odham's curiosity for a desire to hear the religious message they had brought to the new lands. It is more likely that the O'odham wanted to trade with these men for their tools and animals, or to learn practical skills.

O'odham traditions gave them an understanding of the structure of their universe. This included their beliefs about creation, which were much different from Catholic beliefs. Medicine men and head men of each village led O'odham religious ceremonies instead of priests. The effectiveness of the individual medicine man determined his reputation.

Because the O'odham judged a medicine man by his effectiveness, they were perfectly willing to listen to a Jesuit missionary when he came into the villages to teach a better life and a means to salvation after death. When an event such as the baptism of an ill infant seemed to have a healing effect, the O'odham would believe the Christian messages, and at the priest's next appearance, he would be welcomed openly. However, the O'odham also would expect more of him. This happened often with such wanderers as Kino. If subsequent actions failed to produce a desired effect, the priest could lose the prestige he had gained initially.

As the missionaries explored the area, they kept a census of the people they encountered. Kino and his companions estimated that they had visited more than 16,000 O'odham. Since they had not traveled through all of the O'odham lands, one can imagine the lands were populated with considerably more people at that time. Few of the Hia C'eḍ O'odham, for example, would have been included in Kino's account.

Kino found the O'odham pleasant and peaceful for the most part. When he asked his superiors for Jesuit priests to help establish more missions, he told them the O'odham wanted to receive religious instruction. By 1701, the missionaries had arrived in the Tucson area. Although the first one lasted only a year, San Xavier del Bac was finally staffed with a resident priest.

The Spaniards had established a permanent presence in O'odham territory by 1700. The first priests were caring, influential men who seemed to have a genuine concern for the native people. The O'odham began to accept the new circumstances, and they made adjustments, but conditions would change as more Europeans and Mexicans came into the area, and military personnel, missionaries, and settlers invaded the O'odham lands.

# 3

## *A Little Rebellion*

*Darkness reverberates.*
*It rolls me over and over.*
*Beside the singing place I lie down.*
*Darkness reverberates.*

RUTH M. UNDERHILL, *Singing for Power*

When the Spaniards permanently moved into the O'odham lands, they were extremely experienced in dealing with native peoples. They had been exploring America and establishing missions there for nearly two hundred years. The O'odham, on the other hand, did not know what to expect from the Spaniards. This was their first long-term encounter with Europeans and their civilization.

The Spaniards came to the Americas with set ideas about themselves and the native people. They believed that their way of life was superior to any other that they would encounter, and they felt that, as Christians, it was their responsibility to spread their way of life among the Indians.

The Spanish intruders did not consider that they were replacing valuable cultural traits of the people they conquered. They thought the native peoples practiced religions akin to idolatry, or that they had no religion at all. The Spaniards felt that by introducing Christianity, they would save the native people from eternal damnation.

Feelings of superiority also prevented the Spaniards from trying to understand the native peoples and their cultures, and they were unwilling to try to learn anything from people they considered savages. The natives of the Americas probably learned much more about the Spaniards, but they certainly did not like everything they learned.

The O'odham were greatly interested in the Spaniards, their tools, food, and beasts of burden. In fact, trading partners from the south had brought wheat and other European goods to the O'odham long before the Spaniards established missions. The black-robed Jesuits interpreted this interest as desire to hear the message of Christianity. At first, the O'odham understood very little of the Jesuits' motivations.

During Kino's time, the Jesuits were rather successful among the O'odham. Missionaries usually were generous and shared their produce with any and all visitors. They knew that through food they would win friends and influence leaders among different O'odham groups. But after their first experiences with the European-based civilization, most O'odham rejected the mission programs.

There are various reasons for the O'odham's reactions, but two in particular stand out. First, many of the missionaries and settlers who came to the Pimería Alta took the best lands of the O'odham. Second, the settlers and miners who employed the native people often treated them unfairly.

Only the best lands could support people in permanent dwellings, but the missionaries and Spanish settlers monopolized those lands for their own use as fields for crops or grazing. Initially, only the missionaries took the land from the O'odham, but as mining increased, Spanish settlers followed and began to compete with the missions for the most productive areas where there was enough water to maintain fields and raise animals. This forced the O'odham of those areas to leave the lands of their ancestors, and after the O'odham recognized these trends, they no longer unconditionally welcomed the Spaniards.

Although some of the O'odham who had accepted Catholicism stayed to work at the missions or on the farms, many of the O'odham who had lived in these fertile regions lost use of the land completely. This forced them to adopt seasonal migration, as practiced by most of the Tohono O'odham, to find enough food.

Food may not have been as much of a problem for the O'odham who worked on farms, ranches, and in the mines, but they were often exploited by the settlers. In fact, many of the mines used O'odham and other native peoples as slaves. Such employers cared little about "civilizing" the O'odham but simply tried to get as much work from them, with as little expense, as possible.

Other settlers, however, treated the O'odham workers fairly and paid them an adequate wage. Some even tried to instill what the Europeans would consider proper work habits along with those of dress and behavior. In general, though, the O'odham's negative experiences with the settlers undermined what the conscientious missionaries were trying to achieve.

There were other negative aspects of the Spanish way of life for the O'odham. The missionaries were no more effective when it came to healing the sick or bringing good luck than the medicine men, and they (or the military officers) often issued canes of office to converts who were not respected by group members. In general, the O'odham did not appreciate the interference of the Catholic church and the Spanish military in their lives.

Many Spanish practices were contradictory to the O'odham's traditional communal life, including private land ownership and profiting from other people's labor. The O'odham soon learned to keep quiet if they knew where precious metals could be found. Any talk of gold or silver would bring another wave of unsavory miners or treasure seekers.

Around 1730, a Yaqui Indian discovered silver at Arizonac, near Guevavi. Apparently, while he was traveling through the mountains, he noticed silver on the ground. He told a Spanish storekeeper, and word of this strange find spread to settlers in the south. Soon a stampede of miners raced to find bits of this treasure lying on or near the surface in nearly pure form.

Other mines were established in the Pimería Alta, but none as spectacular and accessible as Arizonac. Most were marginally successful at best. Generally, miners were supposed to relinquish one-fifth of their product to the king of Spain, but authorities decided that forcing the small mines to comply was not worth their trouble. No matter how successful a mine, however, the O'odham did not profit at all and received nothing for the minerals taken from their land.

After Kino died in 1711, there was much less missionary activity in the Papaguería. Wars and turmoil in Europe depleted the Spanish treasury, and the monarchy placed less emphasis on converting native peoples in the Americas. Thus, as time went on, there was less support for the missionaries, and without a strong military, the settlers no longer felt safe from attacks by Apaches and Seris. Consequently, the settlers began to move out of the Papaguería.

In 1730, the Spanish population numbered about three hundred people, most of them living on the southeastern borders of the Papaguería. Though some strongholds of the church remained, most, if not all, of the missions supported fewer natives. The number of Indians living at Dolores, which had been Kino's base, had diminished significantly. Only nine families remained. The others had died in epidemics or abandoned the mission. San Ignacio also had lost a great many of its people. Only thirty-two families remained.

In 1730, in all of the Pimería Alta, mission records listed only 1,200 converts. These numbers were not impressive when the church authorities compared them to the successes of other areas in New Spain that had received similar attention.

Fortunately for the O'odham, the thirty or forty years after Kino's death brought less missionary activity and fewer settlers, but the Apache raids continued. By 1735, the Apaches had driven the Sobaipuris from the San Pedro Valley. They also continued to attack villages along the Santa Cruz River and deep into Tohono O'odham lands.

Even the Seris, who had once settled in mission villages, began to attack Spanish settlers. At one point, the Seris were joined by Tepocas, Salineros, and Tiburon Islanders in rebelling against the Spaniards. In 1730, they threatened most of the Spanish settlements near their lands and killed many people. The Seris also attacked the Opatas and the O'odham, particularly those in the Altar Valley. Because these two tribes remained friendly to the Spanish forces, the Seris considered them enemies.

In 1742, the Spaniards established presidios in Pitic and Terrenate to protect the missions and settlers in the north. The base in Terrenate also helped to reduce the pressure of the Apaches on the people in Sonora and Chihuahua.

Although many remained on good terms with the Spanish people, the O'odham received little respect from the missionaries, the settlers, or the military. Particular objects of Spanish scorn were the O'odham of the desert regions, north of the Altar River and west of the Santa Cruz. These O'odham, who firmly held on to their traditional beliefs, did not remain in one village year-round, and they also relied on their own medicine men, whom the Spaniards believed to be sorcerers.

The Spaniards believed the Sobaipuris and the inhabitants of the Altar and San Miguel river areas were much more civilized than the O'odham of the deserts, but around the middle of the eighteenth century, the Sobaipuris near San Xavier del Bac fell into disfavor. They had a reputation for stealing horses to eat, but the O'odham insisted that they had taken the animals from the Apaches, who were said to prefer horseflesh to any other kind of meat.

Although Kino and the early missionaries developed sympathetic attitudes toward the O'odham, the later missionaries and settlers did not always develop those same feelings because the O'odham did not readily accept their beliefs. The O'odham's view of the Spaniards also changed as the novelty of their appearance and material goods wore off.

After a period of little progress in northern Sonora, the Spanish authorities decided to send more missionaries. A Spanish nobleman had died and left part of his estate to the church to finance missions in the region. Unfortunately, the missionaries who arrived in the late 1730s and 1740s did not have the patience and sympathy of the earlier fathers.

The new missionaries expected that because the O'odham had been exposed to Christianity for many years, they should have adopted its principles. Harsh measures were used to enforce conformity to rules and expectations, and the missionaries often whipped the O'odham for any minor offense, and especially for participation in native traditional activities. Because the O'odham did not believe in corporal punishment, they resented this mistreatment even more.

The harsh attitudes of the new fathers increased the agitation among the O'odham, who already harbored resentment toward the missionaries for taking the best lands and excluding people from using them. Private, exclusive ownership of land was not a part of the O'odham's way of life, for their traditions told them that the land was to be open to anyone.

Since the disturbance of 1695 when Father Saeta was killed at Caborca, the Spanish authorities had experienced little trouble from the O'odham. Usually, the O'odham tried to maintain peace, and they were not prone to violence except in defense of their lands and families. There were minor uprisings in 1732 and 1748, but generally the O'odham remained on good terms with the Spaniards, even aiding them in campaigns against less friendly tribes.

When Spanish military forces were struggling to control the Apaches and Seris, they often enlisted peaceful tribes to strengthen their numbers. Opatas and Lower Pimas were often used as auxiliary soldiers. In the rebellions of 1748, however, some Lower Pimas had joined the Seris, so the Spaniards felt none of the Lower Pimas would be reliable allies. As a result, the Spaniards sought the services of the O'odham, and they recruited some four hundred warriors from the Altar and Magdalena valleys under the leadership of Luis Oacpicagigua.

When the Spaniards attempted to remove rebels from Cerro Prieto and Tiburon Island, the campaign was not overly successful, but the O'odham were valiant soldiers who fought on foot where the Spaniards could not—or would not—go with their horses. In fact, the O'odham did most of the fighting.

When the campaign ended, the Spanish officers bestowed honors on Luis Oacpicagigua as the leader of the O'odham warriors, and he returned as the governor and captain-general of the O'odham. Luis therefore assumed that he, not the missionaries, should have authority over the O'odham and their lands. Of course, the missionaries opposed him, and this conflict led to a serious rebellion of the O'odham, and a setback for the missionary effort in northern Sonora.

During the war with the Seris, Luis had witnessed the ineffectiveness of the Spanish forces. His troops had done most of the fighting, and wherever horses could not be used, the Spanish army either could not or would not fight. When he returned to his village and heard of the troubles his people were experiencing with the settlers and missionaries, he decided to take action.

On November 20, 1751, Luis met his people near Saric, a small settlement near the source of the Altar River, and they made plans for a general rebellion against Spanish rule. They agreed that all people supporting the Spaniards should be removed from O'odham lands; the Spanish settlers, their employees, missionaries, soldiers, and converted Indians, of O'odham or other tribes, must leave or face death.

Luis and his people had various reasons to expect success. Only about three hundred people were loyal to the Spanish crown, and not many of them, perhaps a third, could offer resistance. Santa Ana, the largest settlement of Spaniards and mixed-bloods, had fewer than one hundred inhabitants. Most importantly, the presidios were not prepared and certainly not expecting any hostilities. The soldiers of Terrenate were scattered around the area, and many of those at Fronteras were sick. It seemed the perfect time for a rebellion.

Runners traveled to outlying villages to inform the other O'odham about the plan. Luis encouraged them to destroy the Spaniards and their property, and then flee to the Baboquivari Mountains with their families and herds of animals. Luis knew from experience that the Spaniards would be reluctant to fight in the mountains.

The O'odham at Tubutama received the message the same day it was sent, but one of the O'odham who was loyal to the Spaniards immediately informed the settlers and the missionary, Jacob Sedelmayr. Fourteen of the Spaniards and employees joined Sedelmayr and two soldiers to barricade the mission walls.

Then they sent a message to Father Juan Nentvig at Saric, fearing that the O'odham there might be more successful at keeping the rebellion a secret than the Indians at Tubutama had been. Nentvig received the message and rode through the night until he reached Tubutama safely.

The others at the Saric mission, including Nentvig's servants and employees, were not so fortunate. Luis told them the Apaches were about to attack and convinced about twenty people to come to his house for protection. Then Luis and his men burned the house down while guards prevented any from escaping.

Luis and his allies then began to search for Father Nentvig. When they learned that he had left, they pursued him, but they abandoned the chase when they realized capturing him would take too long. Instead, the rebels returned to Saric and attacked the home of the mayordomo, Laureano. He escaped, but his wife and children were killed. The first night of the rebellion, the O'odham killed about twenty-five people.

Early the next morning, Luis and his men attacked the barricaded walls of the mission at Tubutama. Almost a thousand natives joined the attack against Sedelmayr, Nentvig, and the others, and set fire to the church and house.

The threat of O'odham arrows kept the Spaniards and their companions trapped in the mission, but at nightfall, there was a lull in the fighting. No one had been hurt the first day, but they were convinced their luck would not last. The house had nearly been destroyed and no longer offered much protection. They felt they had to get help, so they sent one of the soldiers to Santa Ana, and a loyal Indian to San Ignacio.

The second day brought renewed attack. More O'odham had arrived during the night, so the attacks were of greater intensity, but the men in the mission were able to hold the rebels off. Then, suddenly, the O'odham ceased fighting.

A soldier left the smoldering building to try to round up some horses, but the rebels captured and killed him before the fight resumed with added fury. Two men were severely hurt. Sedelmayr had scalp wounds and flint from an arrow in his arm, and most of the others in the mission were wounded, but they kept fighting.

At sundown, the natives again retreated, and Nentvig and the others took stock of their supplies. They decided they could not survive another day of battle. Leaving behind the two wounded men who probably would not live through the night, they escaped from the mission under cover of darkness. A route on obscure trails enabled them to avoid detection, and after two days, the fathers and their companions reached Santa Ana.

Meanwhile, the O'odham had been causing trouble all along the Altar River and at Sonoita, to the west. At Caborca, a band of O'odham led by the native governor of Pitic killed eleven people, including Father Tomas Tello, some of the people in the village, and the Indian converts employed by the mission. The rebels then moved to Uquitoa, where they killed twenty Spanish sympathizers and burned any property they could not carry away. Elsewhere in the Altar Valley, twenty-five people were killed. To the west, rebels burned the mission at Sonoita and killed the missionary, Father Heinrich Ruhen; his mayordomo, Juan Orosio; and one of Father Ruhen's servants.

North of Saric, the Spaniards and the people who lived with them met a similar fate among the Sobaipuris. At Arivaca, the rebels attacked the Spaniards and the Christianized Indians, and they killed three families and the mayordomo at the Guevavi mission. When neighboring settlers came to bury the dead, the rebels attacked them, too, forcing them to retreat.

When Father Keller at Suamca heard of the rebellion, he feared it would spread and requested soldiers to protect him and the people at the mission. Only five soldiers could be spared, but the missionary at San Xavier feared trouble, so he gathered the soldiers assigned to his mission and rode to Guevavi. Keller and a large group of settlers then traveled on to the military post of Terrenate.

For the O'odham, the rebellion seemed, at first, a success. Most of the Christianized Indians and settlers were removed from their lands. They had killed more than a hundred people who supported the Spaniards, and they had razed a number of churches. They also had confiscated or destroyed large numbers of livestock and other valuables.

Of course, the Spaniards would not allow the situation to remain as it was. The governor of Sinaloa and Sonora, Diego Ortiz Parrilla, had been the military officer in charge of the campaign against the Seris, in which the O'odham under Luis had played such a significant role. He did not relish the idea of fighting a group of Indians he knew so well, not to mention the fact that he would have to confront a leader he respected and honored. Nevertheless, Ortiz Parrilla assembled his available troops and marched toward the Papaguería.

Governor Ortiz Parrilla made San Ignacio his military command post and held a council to determine the cause of the hostilities and how to deal with the situation. Some six hundred Spaniards, Christianized Indians, and mestizos (persons of Spanish and Indian descent) from Santa Ana and the Altar Valley assembled at San Ignacio, but unfortunately, no one was able, or willing, to explain the disturbance.

Although none of the Jesuit priests in the council could comprehend that their behavior had anything to do with the Indians' outrage, they all had suggestions about how to restore peace. Father Stiger of San Ignacio wanted an immediate attack on Tubutama and other areas until all traces of rebellion were wiped out. Then the settlers could return safely to their homes, and Stiger's mission would not have to harbor all of them.

However, the military officers did not agree to take immediate action against the O'odham. They wanted to solve the matter without further bloodshed, and they especially did not want a war against Luis, whom they held in high esteem for serving the Spanish cause in earlier campaigns.

The Jesuits did not share the military's appreciation of Luis because he had not supported them, especially when he had been asked to help improve people's morals. Instead, Luis had encouraged the O'odham to continue living according to their ancient traditions. The fathers also accused Luis of denying their authority and acting arrogantly in his appointed office.

The Jesuit fathers also disliked Pedro Chihuahua, who was the sergeant-general of the Pimas. Months before the uprising, there had been a disagreement over whether Pedro should be allowed to keep his office. When the rebellion broke out, the missionaries were still troubled by the matter and suspected that Pedro was involved in the uprising.

Before Father Keller moved to Terrenate, he wrote to the commanding officer there, Captain Menocal, expressing his suspicion that Pedro was involved in the rebellion. Father Keller suggested that Pedro be tried for conspiracy against the Spaniards, and Captain Menocal arrested Pedro. The officer who interrogated Pedro was convinced that he was one of the leaders of the rebellion, and Captain Menocal ordered Pedro shot and his body hanged in a public place as an example to the rebels.

Menocal then planned an attack on Luis and his forces in the Baboquivari Mountains, but when Governor Ortiz Parrilla arrived at San

Ignacio, he prevented Menocal from continuing with his plan. Just as Menocal was ready to march to the Baboquivari Mountains with Father Keller and the other Jesuit fathers, Ortiz Parrilla ordered him to come to San Ignacio. When Menocal failed to justify his actions against Pedro, the governor sent him to Fronteras and ordered him to remain there and not get further involved.

Ortiz Parrilla then sent emissaries to Luis's camp, where they learned that some of the Gila River Pimas had allied themselves with Luis, and that the rebels were planning to attack Terrenate and San Ignacio. Luis was willing to negotiate with Ortiz Parrilla, but not with the envoys. He demanded that the governor come in person to the talks, but Ortiz Parrilla refused to meet on Luis's terms.

In the meantime, reinforcements arrived from distant presidios, and soon there were 140 soldiers in San Ignacio. But since the O'odham had about 3,000 armed warriors, the governor thought an offensive action would be unwise. They would wait until more troops arrived from the south.

There were continued attempts to negotiate with Luis, but the envoys could not find him. He seemed to have disappeared. Ortiz Parrilla prepared for an attack, but nothing happened. Finally, more troops arrived, and Ortiz Parrilla no longer had reason to delay. Although the governor only had about 200 soldiers, the council already had decided that this was the number of soldiers needed to engage in an attack.

Patrols finally located the rebels, and Ortiz Parrilla again sent soldiers to talk with Luis. On January 2, 1752, the governor ordered that a final attempt at negotiations would be made. If unsuccessful, the army would engage Luis in battle.

Since Luis refused to meet with anyone other than the governor, and Ortiz Parrilla refused to meet with him, Luis chose to fight. He brought 2,000 warriors from the camp in the Baboquivari Mountains and confronted the governor's forces on the morning of January 5. The two forces engaged each other twice that day, with the O'odham losing 46 men, including Luis's son. Of the Spanish forces, only two were wounded.

Some of the O'odham began to return to their rancherías in the west, and Luis moved his camp north in an attempt to solidify an alliance with the Gila River Pimas. Meanwhile, the Spaniards had returned to their base at Terrenate.

In an attempt to prevent the alliance between Luis and the Gila River Pimas, Governor Ortiz Parrilla ordered a campaign against the Indians on the lower Santa Cruz River and the Gila. However, Father Keller convinced the captain leading the campaign to disobey the command, insisting that sixty men could not be effective against the strength of the Sobaipuris and the Gila River Pimas.

Clearly, on the Spanish side, another war was forming between the military command and the Jesuit priests. As with the Pedro affair, Ortiz Parrilla was disturbed by the authority that the fathers gave themselves. He did not think it was a missionary's responsibility to intervene in military or judicial matters.

At the end of February 1752, patrols brought news that most of the Indians were leaving Luis's camp and returning to their homes in the west. The governor then sent more than 130 men to confront Luis in the Santa Catalina Mountains. When they arrived at San Xavier del Bac on March 4, 1752, Bac was deserted, but some of the natives were found not far away, and they insisted that Luis was ready to negotiate.

In preliminary discussions, Luis apparently said that if Keller were recalled from the Pimería Alta, the O'odham would surrender. Although Keller's superior was not convinced that Keller was an obstacle to peace in the region, he ordered Keller to leave. A few days later, Luis gave himself up to the Spanish authorities in Tubac.

After his surrender, Luis blamed the Jesuits for conditions leading to the rebellion. He accused them of using lands set aside for the O'odham, and of severely and unjustly punishing anyone who questioned their commands. Garrucho at Guevavi, Nentvig at Saric, and Keller at Suamca were the most serious offenders, but similar charges were made against other Jesuits throughout the region.

The O'odham also were upset with the mayordomos, who usually were not O'odham. Luis wanted them removed, and all missionaries other than Stiger replaced. The governor seems to have believed Luis because he sent him home without punishment, but Ortiz Parrilla could not promise that the missionaries would be removed.

The governor considered the case closed, and he began preparations to return home. Although the viceroy approved of Ortiz Parrilla's method for ending the hostilities, he insisted that a new presidio be built in the Pimería Alta to discourage future uprisings. Within a year, the Spaniards established a presidio at Tubac. Subsequent investigations of the rebellion exonerated the Jesuits, and eventually the

Spaniards attributed the rebellion to the O'odham's natural love of freedom.

Shortly after he released Luis, Governor Ortiz Parrilla was reassigned to another position. The next governor had Luis arrested because there were continual disturbances in the Papaguería, and within weeks, Luis died in prison in Horcasitas. During the next several years, small groups of O'odham continued to attack missions and settlers, and these rebels probably caused more trouble for the missions during the 1750s than the Apaches did.

Still, the Seris and Apaches continued to be a problem for both the Spaniards and the O'odham. Because some O'odham had joined the Seris' stronghold in the Cerro Prieto, however, the Spanish military did not ask them to help fight the Seris. And even though the rebellion was over, some O'odham refused to give up the fight.

The aftermath of the rebellion changed the Pimería Alta in important ways. In particular, the Spaniards completely or partly abandoned many of their larger and more desirable settlements, including Santa Ana, Ocuca, San Xavier del Bac, Arivaca, Guevavi, Sonoita, and Tumacacori. This was an advantage for the O'odham, of course, but only for a decade or two.

Apaches were still raiding both the Spanish settlements and the O'odham villages. In 1771, the Apaches attacked Aquimuri and killed all the people—men, women, and children—burned all the buildings, and stole all the food. Four years later, the Apaches encouraged the O'odham to join them in a revolt against the Spaniards. Though the O'odham revealed the plot to the Spaniards, the authorities took no action against the Apaches. In November 1775, a group of Seris and Apaches attacked the mission at Magdalena, destroyed buildings, drove off cattle, and killed a woman.

The Apaches also attacked Saric and killed eleven converts. Although they did not destroy the church, they wreaked havoc similar to the destruction suffered at Magdalena. Continuing attacks in subsequent years completely depopulated the village by 1828. The wealthier Spaniards moved their families and livestock to less dangerous areas. This would have been to the advantage of the O'odham except they then became the main target of Apache attacks.

With continued Apache problems in the north, the viceroy of New Spain, Bernardo Galvez, decided a new tactic should be used to establish and maintain peace. After 1789, he strengthened the military garrisons and promised the Apaches gifts of food, alcohol, and weapons if they would settle down and cease their attacks on the settlers and the more peaceful Indian tribes.

The combination of a stronger military presence and bribery diminished the threats from the Apaches. The activity of missionaries and settlers also decreased, so the O'odham enjoyed relative peace for the last three decades that they were nominally under the jurisdiction of Spain. Although the O'odham were still called upon to counter an occasional Apache attack, these occurred less frequently, and the Spanish military provided greater protection and a means of retribution.

The Spaniards had sent another group of Jesuits to the Pimería Alta in the mid-1750s, and even though most of them were Germans, they were sent in the service of the Catholic church and the Spanish monarchy. These fathers joined those who had remained after the rebellion, and they continued their work, trying to convert and control the O'odham. Some of the O'odham did move to the mission villages, where they planted crops and took care of the animals, but only a few converted to Catholicism. Then, in 1767, Spanish authorities expelled the Jesuits from Spanish lands, not because of their actions toward the O'odham or other native peoples, but as a result of political upheavals in Spain. The Catholic church subsequently assigned Franciscan monks to take the places of the departing Jesuits.

In the one to three years before the Franciscans staffed the missions, the O'odham who had converted to Christianity often abandoned the missions to rejoin their families. When the Franciscans arrived, they diligently worked to bring order to the missions once again. Some began exploring new areas, and one, Father Garcés, established a reputation as Kino's successor. Father Garcés traveled throughout O'odham lands and northward into what is now central Arizona and established contact with O'odham groups and other tribes in the region.

The Europeans brought more than religion and culture to the Americas. They also brought devastating diseases that periodically ravaged the native populations. Measles, chicken pox, and new strains of flu destroyed entire communities because most native peoples had no immunity to such diseases. Old and young perished in the epidemics. Periodic bouts of smallpox also killed many people.

The population of the O'odham seems to have declined considerably during the eighteenth century, but it is hard to determine exact figures. In the 1730s, the villages of Dolores and Remedios had severe smallpox epidemics, and in 1760, a flu-like disease killed and disabled many people. Another unknown illness struck in 1765 and destroyed entire families.

In 1703, Kino estimated that 16,000 people lived in the Pimería Alta, 7,000 of whom were Sobaipuris. Sixty years later, missionaries estimated the population had decreased by half. The Apaches had pushed the Sobaipuris to the Santa Cruz Valley and beyond, and they were losing their identity as a separate group as many of them died from disease or intermarried with the other O'odham groups.

The Europeans moved permanently into the O'odham lands during the eighteenth century, and although they did not move to the heart of the Papaguería, they settled much of the southeastern region. They also had missions in the east, but Apaches prevented much settlement to the north.

As it turned out, the O'odham's rebellion against the heavy-handed encroachment of Europeans gained them nothing. Many O'odham had been forced by Apache and European intruders to retreat from areas they had formerly used, and they suffered terribly from disease. However, for most O'odham, life continued much the way it had for centuries.

# 4

## Minor Changes, Major Problems

*Oh, bitter wind, keep blowing*
*That therewith my enemy*
*Staggering forward*
    *Shall fall.*

*Oh, bitter wind, keep blowing*
*That therewith my enemy*
*Staggering sideways*
    *Shall fall.*

RUTH M. UNDERHILL, *Papago Woman*

The O'odham witnessed the Jesuits' expansion of the mission system in the Pimería Alta as far north and west as it would ever extend. The Franciscans hoped to establish new missions on the Gila and Colorado rivers, and among the O'odham in the west, but for the most part, they were unsuccessful. This was partly because the Spanish government could no longer afford to support the mission system or the military on the northern frontiers. But it was also because the O'odham were much less interested in the missionaries than they had been before.

Although more Franciscans than Jesuits came to O'odham lands, they were not as successful as the Jesuits in attracting new converts and opening new missions. Still, the Franciscans continued to maintain the mission system and added many impressive church buildings to O'odham lands.

For those who converted to Catholicism and remained on the missions, the missions provided a means for subsistence and religious instruction. Unfortunately for the Franciscans, at the end of the eighteenth century, the Spanish government no longer wanted to support the missions. The government considered the missions too expensive for the little that they accomplished compared to more developed areas than the Pimería Alta.

A mission was deemed successful when it could become a parish with many believers who attended services regularly, like the parishes in Europe. The Franciscans, as well as others familiar with conditions on the northern frontier, knew that developing such parishes would take years because the O'odham were not entirely converted to either the Spanish economic system or the Catholic church.

Those O'odham who accepted the Spanish religion and way of life received land from the mission for their own use. In return for the privilege of working their own fields, converts had to work three days each week on the mission fields. In this way, they maintained the missions and, in turn, the missions gave them a secure source of food.

But only a few O'odham embraced the Catholic religion and lived on the missions. Most did not consider the missions permanent dwelling places, but came to the missions only for the planting and harvesting seasons or in times of need because the missions had surplus food and opportunities for work.

Some mission records from the late eighteenth century show that burials outnumbered baptisms by as many as twenty to one. This indicates that many families were not living at the missions, nor were they coming to the mission to have their children baptized. When the early Jesuits opened the missions, the O'odham had many more of their children baptized. Perhaps they later felt that baptisms were less effective for protecting their children than their traditional medicine. Most left the missions and raised their children elsewhere.

At the same time, however, records seem to indicate that the O'odham relied on missions as a refuge for the elderly and the infirm. Most likely the people saw missions as sanctuaries for those unable to take care of themselves in the desert. Life at the missions was easier, and food and shelter were available throughout the year.

Sickness was common among the O'odham and severely depleted the population of many O'odham groups. Like many other native peoples, they took a long time to develop immunity to European diseases. As more and more Spaniards and others moved into the Altar River valley and along the upper Santa Cruz River, the risk of being exposed to new diseases increased, and a great many O'odham died. Many of those who did survive moved farther into the Papaguería to join the Tohono O'odham, the people of the desert.

By the late 1700s and the early 1800s, numerous deaths and continued migration into the more remote regions had erased many of the differences that had distinguished the various groups of O'odham.

Missionaries noted that as the Sobas and Sobaipuris on their missions died, they were replaced by the Papagos. "Papago" was the name the Spaniards gave to the native people who spoke the Piman language and lived in the arid region west of the Santa Cruz Valley, between the Altar Valley and the Gila River. This included the Tohono and the Hia C'eḍ O'odham to the north and to the west. With the exception of the Gila River Pimas, the Spanish considered all the northern Pimas "Papagos."

The O'odham west of the Santa Cruz Valley generally moved at least twice a year and had less opportunity to establish irrigated fields and year-round residences than their cousins who lived along the rivers. The Hia C'eḍ O'odham, who lived west of what is now Ajo, were the least settled of the O'odham and more or less maintained a separate identity.

By 1800, the Sobaipuris were no longer a separate group of the O'odham, although some individuals claimed to be Sobaipuris until late in the century. As a result of the Spanish policy of relocating Indians, and the continuing attacks by Apaches, the Sobaipuris were removed or driven from the San Pedro River drainage to the villages of the Gila River Pimas or to the Santa Cruz River near Bac and Tucson. There and farther west, they began to mix with the Tohono O'odham and eventually became indistinguishable from them.

The O'odham in the southern region had experienced a similar fate. When the Spaniards first came to the Pimería Alta, their encroaching missions and settlers pushed the O'odham to less desirable lands. Eventually, they assimilated into the desert dwelling groups or accepted Spanish culture. Of those who did remain in their original lands, some joined the missions while others adopted Spanish methods of land use and ownership. Often, O'odham intermarried with people of European descent or of mixed European–Native American descent. Some married other native peoples who had moved north to seek new lands after they had adopted the Spanish culture—or lost lands to the Spaniards. Many descendants of those who intermarried with other people eventually lost their identity as O'odham.

The Apaches were yet another major factor in the blending of the various bands of O'odham. Although the desert region was not attractive to the Spaniards or to the native people who had accepted their culture, this sparse land still provided what was needed for life. Unfortunately, the Apaches knew this and raided the desert villages for food, supplies, and captives.

These raids substantially changed the O'odham way of life. The Apaches forced them to become increasingly more defensive and to assemble in larger groups, eliminating the satellite communities in which small bands had lived. Although gathering enough food to support larger populations was more difficult, larger villages were necessary for protection from the Apaches.

Even the Hia C'eḍ O'odham worried about Apache raids. The so-called Sand People lived far to the west, often in the desert sand dunes, but Apaches reached at least part of their lands. Following the Gila River west from their homelands, the Apaches swept through the area where Ajo is now located, but the Hia C'eḍ O'odham were sometimes difficult to find and had few possessions the Apaches wanted.

Fortunately for the O'odham, Spanish settlements were much more attractive to the Apaches. Because of their farming systems and market economy, the settlers and missions had large herds of animals and storage bins filled with grain. This abundance of food was much more attractive to the Apaches than the meager subsistence fare of the O'odham, and the Apaches directed most of their raids southward, striking in Sonora as far south as what is now Hermosillo. The Apaches and Comanches even attacked villages within two hundred miles of Mexico City.

The Apaches had become a menace to all of the northern provinces of New Spain, and in the late 1780s, Spanish authorities used a new approach to subdue them. They negotiated peace treaties with some bands by promising to supply food, alcohol, and animals, and they also gave the Apaches obsolete arms and ammunition, assuming that the Indians would be dependent upon the Spaniards for maintenance of the weapons and supplies of ammunition.

At that time, however, the arrows used by the Apaches were more devastating to the Spaniards than the Spanish guns were to the Apaches. An Apache could launch about ten arrows in the time it took a Spanish soldier to reload and fire another shot. The Spaniards reasoned that if the Apaches would use firearms, the soldiers would be on an equal, or even superior, footing with the Apaches.

When Apache bands refused to submit to a treaty, the military forces of New Spain relentlessly pursued them until they agreed to cooperate—or were destroyed or captured. The Spaniards sent captives to Mexico City at first, then decided that Cuba was better because they could not easily escape and return home. This new approach enabled the Spaniards to establish some peace on the northern frontier from around 1785 to the mid-1820s.

Although the O'odham had less to fear from their traditional enemies, the respite from Apache attacks allowed settlers to move into O'odham lands once again. Farmers and miners renewed activities that they had abandoned during the dangerous years, and the O'odham watched as these intruders took more and more traditional lands for their own use.

But the O'odham were not the only people affected by the new wave of settlement. The missions, located in some of the best farming and grazing areas, became the envy of people moving in. These Spaniards, or Spanish Americans, felt that the missions were temporary institutions to help the Indians become self-sustaining, tax-paying citizens. For years, missions had been stabilizing elements that allowed settlers to move safely into an area, but ironically, the settlers eventually wanted to eliminate the missions so more land would be available to them.

Because the missions were costly, the Spanish government agreed with the settlers on at least one point: the missions should remain for as little time as possible. But the O'odham did not adopt Spanish ways as rapidly as many other Indian tribes to the south. The forces of assimilation were not as strong on the frontier, and most of the O'odham avoided the missions and settlers except when food was scarce or when they wanted to trade their goods. Many who did reside on or near the missions died from diseases and thus did not pass the European cultural influence on to their children or the people outside the mission.

The government in Mexico City wanted to close the missions as soon as possible, but the missionaries argued against that, claiming the O'odham had not reached a point where they could become citizens and compete with the settlers. The missionaries felt that if they forced the O'odham to become citizens before they were ready, the O'odham would rapidly revert to the lifeways they had before mission supervision influenced them.

In reality, however, the O'odham had not been strongly influenced and had managed to avoid forced acceptance of European domination longer than most of the native peoples in Sonora. After their initial acceptance of the early Kino missions, most O'odham did not choose to live with the Europeans or to adopt a new way of life.

The O'odham living in the desert were much less influenced by the Spaniards than those living in the river valleys. Aside from borrowing food crops, using horses, and trading for tools and cooking implements, they lived much as their ancestors had lived for centuries. The occasional visitor who wandered through their lands looking for mineral wealth to exploit or a favorable site to farm was little more than a curiosity. In the eighteenth century, no important mines were developed west of the Santa Cruz Valley.

The Spaniards had much more influence over the O'odham who remained close to the settlers. Those who accepted work at the missions and in the settlers' fields at planting and harvesting time received wages and became familiar with a cash economy. They also had to learn Spanish to work with the missionaries and settlers because few of the newcomers learned the native languages.

Some O'odham came in close contact with the Spaniards through military service. The O'odham were valiant soldiers, a more formidable foe of the Apaches than either the Spanish military or the settlers, and because of this, Spanish military officials often recruited them. The Seris feared the O'odham warriors more than any other troops (although sometimes the O'odham fought with the Seris against the settlers).

The O'odham recruited by the military became accustomed to many aspects of Spanish culture. First and foremost, they learned Spanish in order to understand the commands of their military leaders (some of whom were natives trained by the Spaniards). They also ate food supplied by the Spaniards and cooked to European tastes, and they lived and worked in buildings of European design. Eventually, they also learned to ride horses and use European weapons.

The military employed some eighty O'odham warriors, but like most other soldiers, they seldom received any money. This was because of the military wage policy. Soldiers were responsible for providing their own food, ammunition, and other supplies, but the officers purchased these things and sold them to the soldiers, usually at inflated prices. The officers then kept the soldiers' wages to pay their bills. It usually worked out that the soldiers saw little of the money they had earned, and they often were in debt.

In 1782, the Spanish military established a company of O'odham soldiers at San Ignacio, and by 1787, the company had moved to Tubac. Tubac was a major outpost in the defense against Apaches traveling south to attack Sonoran villages and missions. Other soldiers had been ineffective against the Apaches, but even though (or perhaps because) they used native weapons, the O'odham were more successful. After 1785, the new policy for pacifying Apaches began to take effect, and the O'odham soldiers had little more to do than prepare for a reoccurrence of hostilities.

Meanwhile, the Franciscans hoped to expand their missions to include all the O'odham (or Papagos, as they were called), the Gila River Pimas, and the Yuma Indians on the Colorado River. However, they never established a mission among the Pima, and their efforts on the Colorado River ended in disaster. The Yuma Indians massacred the settlers who went there to establish a mission, and the renowned Fray Garcés was among the victims.

Garcés's death in July 1781 was a major setback for the missionaries, and especially disheartening. The native people respected him, and unlike most Franciscans, he had attempted to learn the O'odham language. Garcés had helped develop a land route to California, and he was involved with Anza's expedition to colonize Monterrey Bay and to establish the presidio at San Francisco. He also explored some of the O'odham lands that Kino had visited, and he explored the Colorado River to the Bill Williams Fork, and much of the interior of what is now Arizona, even reaching the Hopi villages.

However, the wars in Europe severely depleted Spain's financial resources. As a result, the Franciscan missionaries received little money, and thus their efforts to establish missions on the northern frontier were thwarted. The O'odham in the desert were more or less left to themselves.

Still, the missionaries sometimes were able to entice some of the O'odham to the missions. In 1796, one such group from the ranchería of Aquituni agreed to move to Tucson, which was a *visita* (a branch of a parish or a mission that a priest or missionary visited) of the San Xavier del Bac mission. The missionaries promised them certain privileges, such as land and water use and access to food that the missionaries had stored. A drought in the previous months had made the lives of the O'odham particularly difficult, and this encouraged 134 of the people living at Aquituni to move to Tucson.

Unfortunately, trouble broke out immediately. The soldiers and settlers from the presidio and the community across the river took most of the water from the Santa Cruz River, leaving only a trickle for these recruits. In addition, soldiers and settlers allowed their horses and cattle to graze in O'odham fields. Realizing that there was no future there without trouble, the group returned to the desert.

Father Llorens, a missionary at San Xavier, then persuaded the group to move to his mission. However, when the commandant general learned of this, he decreed that the missionaries were not allowed to bring any more natives to San Xavier del Bac. There were two reasons for this. First, the San Xavier mission was upstream from the Tucson presidio. If more people moved there, the water supply would diminish for the settlers at Tucson. Second, if the O'odham settled on the favorable lands around the San Xavier mission, they would keep the Spanish settlers from expanding into the area. Naturally, under such circumstances, the O'odham felt less than welcome at the missions, and they usually were more content to remain in the desert and avoid contact with the settlers and troops.

Although the treaties with the Apaches benefited the O'odham and the Spanish settlers, the peace was not complete. The Apaches still took advantage of opportunities to attack. Many never were caught because the Apache bands did not stay in one place where the Spanish military could monitor their activities.

For example, on June 5, 1801, Apaches attacked the mission at Tumacacori and killed three men who had been tending flocks outside the mission walls. The next day, troops and settlers from nearby Tubac arrived and drove the Apaches from the mission. However, before they departed, the Apaches slaughtered the mission flock, leaving some 1,360 sheep lying in the fields. Regardless of occasional Apache attacks, the relative peace in northern Sonora attracted many new settlers, and during the first two decades of the nineteenth century, there was a large influx of settlers into the Pimería Alta. Town populations fluctuated considerably, however, because farming and mining jobs were seldom consistent and rarely permanent.

Then, in 1816, a flu epidemic ravaged northern Sonora. Mission records indicate that many people died, with some towns losing up to 25 percent of their inhabitants. In many villages, more than 50 percent of the victims were children under the age of fifteen. Because missionaries were the only source of such records, and most O'odham lived outside of the missions, no records exist to indicate how the epidemic affected them.

The relative peace with the Apaches that encouraged settlers to move into the Upper Pimería also allowed the O'odham to form smaller groups again and disperse themselves across the land. Family groups separated from the larger units created for mutual defense, making food-gathering more efficient and productive, especially in outlying communities where they could farm the alluvial deposits as their ancestors had done for centuries. Some O'odham who began to raise cattle also found that it was better to spread out so their herds would not compete for forage, but with the exception of cattle-raising, the O'odham returned to a more traditional life after the threat of Apache attack had diminished.

Although the O'odham were unaware of policies made by the Spaniards, they often felt the effects. For example, they experienced fewer Apache raids after the Spaniards negotiated treaties with the Apaches, but few, if any, of the O'odham knew why the Apaches had become more peaceful.

Similarly, the O'odham were generally unaware of political events involving the American colonies, yet the colonies' movement toward independence ultimately had a significant influence on the lives of the O'odham. Two events that greatly affected their future were the Revolutionary War and the Mexican war for independence.

The Revolutionary War separated the British colonies in North America from Great Britain in 1783 and created the United States. The Mexican wars finally secured independence for Mexico in 1821.

The Revolutionary War was important for many reasons. The Spanish and the French joined forces to support the American colonists in their fight against Great Britain because both countries wanted to break British control of the colonies and weaken British power worldwide. In the end, however, that support hurt the Spanish empire.

Spain spent a great deal of money in the wars against Great Britain, which ultimately weakened the Spanish empire. Also, the policies of the newly created United States allowed for a westward expansion that could not be stopped. Additionally, the success of the United States in gaining independence inspired American colonists in Spanish-controlled areas to rebel against their mother country, Spain.

Because the Revolutionary War had drained much of Spain's financial resources, the Spanish government neglected the frontier regions of New Spain. Military personnel were needed elsewhere, and the frontier had to be guarded by less experienced soldiers. This left the frontiers vulnerable to settlement by foreigners, in particular citizens of the newly formed United States.

Under British control, the colonists had been prohibited from moving beyond the Appalachian Mountains. However, with the formation of the United States, restrictions were removed, and many people rapidly moved westward. First, they settled the lands east of the Mississippi River because Great Britain had ceded that territory to the former colonies in the treaty that ended the colonists' war for independence. Then, after the United States negotiated the Louisiana Purchase with France in 1803 and obtained the land west of the Mississippi River to the Rocky Mountain crest (except for Mexican-claimed Texas), settlers began to move into the entire western region as well.

The U.S. citizens did not stop at the borders of their land. They continued westward, ignoring the claims of Spain and England. They usually took what they wanted without regard for those who were already using the land, and they seemed to have less respect for the rights of the native peoples than the Spanish settlers did.

Under Spanish law, the native people had rights of citizenship and legal protection. Although the settlers often ignored these rights, at least the possibility of protection was there. In contrast, the Indians had no rights under U.S. law, and few settlers respected their claims to the land.

By setting in motion this unrestrained westward migration, the Revolutionary War forever changed the lives of the O'odham and all other native peoples. Within a half century, U.S. explorers, fur traders, farmers, and ranchers had ventured into and through the northern half of New Spain.

In 1808, a movement toward independence began in New Spain, and when Napoleon deposed Ferdinand VII of Spain, Spanish authority in the colonies became unstable. The Spanish colonists seized the moment to claim their independence, but this initial attempt failed because competing groups could not decide who should have power once the new country was formed.

Two years later, Miguel Hidalgo y Costilla, a priest from the Bajía, led another attempt to free Mexico from Spanish control. The rebels took over Guadalajara but failed to advance to the capital city. Eventually, the smaller but well-disciplined Spanish army led by Felix Cajeta defeated the much larger, disorganized army of rebels.

Rebels continued subversive activities within New Spain, constantly pushing for independence. Another priest, José María Morelos, carried on the fight until Spanish loyalists captured and executed him in December 1815. After his execution, the focus of the rebellion shifted to the southern region of New Spain, where guerrillas kept the embers of revolution warm.

In 1820, a revolution in Spain forced the king to accept a liberal constitution limiting the power and influence of the Catholic church, and high church officials in New Spain began to consider Mexican independence as a means to preserve their traditional role.

At this time, rebels in the south were conducting guerrilla warfare from the mountains, and the viceroy of New Spain appointed Augustín Iturbide to end the conflict. Iturbide had been instrumental in the defeat of Morelos but because of the revolution in Spain, his allegiance to the royalist cause was no longer strong.

On February 26, 1821, Iturbide made public his plans for the independence of Mexico, and the guerrillas later overcame their suspicions about Iturbide's intentions and joined with his forces. Other royalist officers also followed Iturbide's example. Without authority to maintain his power, the viceroy of New Spain decided to resign. The independence of Mexico had been achieved, and New Spain no longer existed.

Independence did not solve the country's problems, however, and in fact left the new government with fewer resources to meet the country's needs. The Mexican people could no longer look to Spain for financial or military assistance. Also, economic production, which had been falling since 1805, reached just 50 percent of its 1805 level after independence. Mexico was born in poverty, and it would remain in that condition for years to come. It was not until the 1870s that the country reached the production levels achieved under the Spanish government in 1805.

To the people of the northern frontier of Sonora, and the O'odham in particular, independence had very little meaning, even though it later had important consequences for them. Traditional life on the frontier continued undisturbed. Even the formation of a state joining Sonora to Sinaloa caused no concern among the native peoples of the Pimería Alta.

Under Spanish law, native peoples granted citizenship held the same rights as any other citizen. In practice, however, New Spain functioned under a class system based on racial differences, in which native peoples fell on the low end of the social register.

According to the Mexican constitution, however, all people were equal citizens of the state with the same rights and responsibilities. A citizen had the right to own land, but he also had to pay taxes to support the government. This concept of private property was foreign to the tradition of most Indian tribes in northern Mexico, but during colonization, the Spanish government established missions to teach the Indians the European system of land use and ownership. The Spaniards hoped that once the Indians accepted these methods, they would become productive, tax-paying citizens along with the immigrants and the natives in the south.

After independence, the new country of Mexico had difficulty maintaining a stable government, partly due to the lack of a productive economy that would support the government's programs. The years of turmoil before and after independence crippled the economy and left Mexico without the means to continue the programs that the Spanish government had funded.

For the O'odham, Mexico's financial problems were the major effect of independence because the new Mexican government no longer could support the presidios. The presidios were the northern defense system against the attacks of hostile Indians, and troops also monitored the intrusions of U.S. citizens. But Mexico did not have enough money to maintain an effective military force on the frontier or support the work of the missions, nor could it pacify the Apaches with gifts of food and supplies.

Only a small number of O'odham who were associated with the mission or the military were affected directly by these changes, but the Mexican government's inability to control the Apaches had a considerable effect on the Papaguería. The Apaches were not going to remain settled long if the government did not continue to meet the conditions of their treaties.

The first two decades of the nineteenth century brought many changes to Spain and New Spain. Revolution had forced Spanish rulers to adopt a liberal constitution. The independence of the British colonies in North America created a new nation, the United States, that expanded west and altered Spain's empire in North America, and New Spain experienced similar turmoil created by its own independence movement. After all the strife, Mexico became a new nation in 1821.

Through all of this, little had changed for the O'odham in the Papaguería, and they continued to live much as their ancestors had. The O'odham did adopt new foods, metal implements, and horses, which brought significant changes, and some groups of the O'odham to the south and to the east had died from disease and the attacks of hostile Apaches. Others had lost their identity as O'odham as they were assimilated into other groups of people. Still others had moved into the desert to avoid those problems. However, the O'odham living in the inner regions of the traditional lands remained relatively unaffected by the European intrusion.

# 5

## Encirclement

*1848—In this year happened an almost unbelievable thing. Cold*
*weather of unheard-of intensity swooped down on the Papagos and*
*almost snuffed them out. Snow fell to a depth of three feet on the level*
*and as deep as the tops of houses in drifts, and lay on the ground for*
*many weeks. Cattle and horses could not find food under the snow*
*and the People could not find firewood. There was great suffering*
*because the People had always been accustomed to warm winters.*
Calendar stick deciphered by Sevilla Juan, 1936
*The Papago Indian Reservation and the Papago People*
William M. Tatom, ed.

The four decades following Mexican independence were very important for the O'odham. The Mexican government was very unstable;
only a few administrations lasted more than a year or two. With such
instability at the highest levels of government, it was difficult to for-
mulate any consistent policy to deal with the northern frontier.

The instability of the Mexican government extended also to state
and local governments. There was constant debate over what form the
government should take and where political power should be focused.
The centrists thought that most power should be centered in the national government in Mexico City. The federalists, who thought that
most power should reside with the individual state governments, opposed the centrists. This quarrel kept Mexico and its states in turmoil
for half a century.

The O'odham were not concerned with the problems of Mexican
politicians most of the time. Occasionally, a politician would ask for
help, and groups of O'odham warriors would engage in battles for
power between rival factions. The primary motivation for such involvement was money; political rivals often recruited native people
with offers of wages or other rewards for fighting.

From 1839 to 1840, fighting in Mexico was severe. One O'odham
record keeper was so impressed with the fighting that he began a
calendar stick, an aid to help the recorder remember events. The

notches that the stick keeper makes in the stick remind him of the events, which he later recalls and then teaches to the subsequent record keeper. Ruth Underhill, an anthropologist of the 1930s, recorded the translation of one stick keeper's initial entry: "1839–40—This was the year when 'the world went wrong.' There was fighting in Mexico. . . . During the hottest part of the summer a Papago named Take-a-Horse killed an Enemy."

The constant political turmoil adversely affected the missions, and the O'odham who lived on them suffered from this instability. No one knew exactly what to do with the mission system. It had been a part of the Mexican heritage almost since the Europeans first arrived, but missions were expensive to run, and the new Mexican government did not have the funds to support them. Even before Mexican independence, the monarchy in Spain had found the missions a severe financial burden. Also, voluntary contributions from wealthy benefactors in Spain and other countries in Europe ceased after Mexico became free.

Lack of money was not the only problem facing the missions, however. Settlers who were intruding into the region wanted the missions' lands. The missionaries had chosen and maintained the best farming and grazing lands, but because officials did not always have documentation of legal title, they often found it difficult to prove what land belonged to them. Boundary markers were often trees that had since died, or rocks that had disappeared, and descriptions of the lines were often vague or inexact. Written documentation frequently was lost, destroyed—or perhaps never produced because there had been no need earlier to prove claim to the land.

Although some O'odham had fields on or near the missions, they often lost lands because they did not understand the legal system and had no proof of ownership. If they left to visit relatives or to gather food, a settler might arrive and decide the land was vacant because no one was on it at the time.

The government had an interest in lands being privately owned. The O'odham on the missions were not required to pay taxes, and those who lived off the missions seldom raised more than they needed to survive. Surplus was usually traded rather than sold for cash. Since the O'odham seldom earned money, the state could not tax them, but in contrast, the ranchers and farmers who produced profitable harvests contributed to the economy and produced revenues for the state in the form of taxes.

The missions also came under attack as protectors of Indian rights. Although most of the Franciscans in the northern Sonoran missions were from Spain, and were usually supporters of the king and of Spanish rule, after independence, most of them remained at their appointed posts. They wanted to help their converts remain true to their new beliefs and, in some cases, to help them retain their lands. Also, they had to receive directions from their religious order in order to move.

The politicians of Sonora wavered in their support for the missions. In the mid-1820s, Governor Simon Elias Gonsález wanted to establish new missions in the lands of the Gila Pimas and thus extend Mexican control farther northward. However, Gonsález lacked finances to attempt this plan. Other governors allowed Mexican settlers to take mission lands. These settlers also stole mission and O'odham water and herds of animals. They ignored the laws and rights of both the Indians and the missions.

The national government did little to assist the missions either. The government never had enough money to support the missions anyway, but they were also a reminder of Spanish colonialism. The missions did not fit into the modern concept of the Mexican state, which advocated equality and freedom among all citizens as well as separation of church and state. Finally, in 1828, Comandante de Armas Mariano Paredes expelled the Spanish friars, insisting without foundation that the friars had incited the Native Americans to rebel. He then placed the missions in the hands of salaried civilians, who were responsible for maintaining them.

However, the civilian managers sold much of the valuable land and either consumed the animals or sold them for their own profit. They also abused the O'odham, took away their privileges, and drove many of them away from the mission lands.

These actions destroyed the missions and imperiled the towns that had developed around them. No longer could the missions attract the O'odham, who tried to avoid the intruding settlers.

In 1830, a new regime came to power in Mexico and returned what remained of the missions to the Mexican-born Father President José María Perez Llera. Father Llera was a Franciscan who had remained in Sonora, and he and two or three other friars (none of whom had connections to Spain) tried to reestablish the missions—and regain the O'odham's acceptance of the mission system itself.

A Mexican law in 1833 nationalized much of the church property and did away with the missions in most of Mexico, but the problems faced by the missions on the Sonoran frontier made them so unattractive that they were exempt from the law. The local bishop had no desire to assume control either. The missions were impoverished and still menaced by Apaches, and there was a shortage of priests to establish parishes.

However, despite the pleas from Father Llera to the government in Mexico City, the missions could not be rejuvenated. The back of the mission system—which had been in place in upper Sonora since Father Kino established his mission at Dolores in 1687—had been broken. The mission system, the first institution charged with bringing Christianity and European culture to the O'odham, died in 1842 when the Franciscans gave up the missions to a bishop who did not want them.

The missions to the O'odham were never as successful as those to native peoples farther south. Only in the southern and eastern regions of the Pimería Alta did they exert much influence, and even there, not many of the O'odham joined and remained faithful followers of the Catholic church.

Most O'odham were not influenced by the missions or other Spanish intruders. Some who did join the Catholic church shared their faith with members of their bands, but then they were left without supervision, which led to the development of Sonoran Catholicism. Converts usually assimilated into the villages or ranches of the settlers and lost their identities as O'odham.

Regardless of their lack of success and eventual demise, the missions did serve the O'odham well in many respects. Missionaries brought new foods that the O'odham readily accepted and learned to grow. Missions also hired the O'odham to work in exchange for food or trading goods. Also, for a hundred years, the missions had been centers for relief during difficult times.

The missions also encouraged the O'odham to abandon traditional food-gathering in favor of farming. This influence was most prominent in the southeast area of the Pimería Alta, where settlers later pushed out many of those who had been influenced by the missions. However, some O'odham remained. The farming methods they had learned at the missions allowed them to grow more than they used, and they were able to sell the surplus, often to the miners who had moved into region.

The missions also reduced the number of Apache raids on the O'odham. The Apaches attacked the missions often because their herds and storage facilities were attractive targets. Although the O'odham still had to be wary, there were fewer raids after the Mexicans moved into the area.

The missions were also a buffer against the incursions of settlers. The missionaries used whatever legal means they had to keep the settlers from cheating the O'odham, and although they were not always successful in preventing abuses, they did advocate the rights of Indians.

By 1842, the missions had served their purpose, and conditions made it impossible for them to continue the work they had been commissioned to perform. The missions had introduced the Catholic tradition, and as time went on, many O'odham accepted Catholicism or the Sonoran version of it.

With the mission influence and control gone, the bureaucrats of the civil government would now be responsible to attend to the needs and rights of the O'odham as far as the intruding powers were concerned. The O'odham, of course, would have preferred to be left alone.

During the turbulent 1820s, the Apaches began to get restless. Promises received in treaties after 1785 were not being fulfilled. Newly independent Mexico was too poor to fulfill promises made by the Spanish government, and the instability of the Mexican government made the northern frontier a low priority.

Although the raids were infrequent at first, the Apaches began attacking the missions and villages in northern Mexico again, and the Mexican government was powerless against them. The presidios created by the officials of New Spain to protect the frontier were too weak to prevent the Apaches from renewing the attacks, even when they raided far into Mexico.

By the 1830s, the Apaches were conducting full-scale raids, striking missions and towns in the far south of Sonora. However, to the Mexicans, the problems with Texas and the intrusions into Mexican territory by U.S. citizens were more important. The Mexican government let the state of Sonora fend for itself. The O'odham again had to move into defensive villages and abandon the outlying rancherías.

In the 1840s, Apache raids forced people out of the upper and middle Santa Cruz Valley, and attacks in 1848 led to the abandonment of the Tubac presidio and the mission at Tumacacori. A calendar stick transcribed for Underhill records that in 1848, many children died of an unnamed disease, and that the O'odham had gone to Sonora to harvest beans for the Mexicans. There they fought with "the Enemy," as the O'odham called the Apaches, and each side suffered deaths in the fighting. The remainder of the record is replete with accounts of their battles.

The attacks caused wholesale abandonment of ranches and farms and left considerable legal problems regarding land tenure that had to be worked out after the United States gained control over the area. The O'odham who had claims to Tumacacori lost all their lands because they had no legal documentation to verify their ownership. The Apache attacks caused some residents of Tucson and San Xavier del Bac to leave. However, with the influx of the former residents of Tubac and Tumacacori, their populations remained stable, and they became the main population centers along the Santa Cruz River.

The discovery of gold in California led to an exodus from northern Sonora. Although some returned after the gold rush fever had died down, by the end of the 1840s, as many as ten thousand people had left Sonora. Among them were soldiers who had abandoned the presidios to look for gold, further diminishing the already weak defense of the frontier.

The Apache raids continued until the 1880s and 1890s, when the U.S. Army rounded up the Apaches and placed them on reservations. By then, however, Anglo-Americans from the United States had moved into the area.

Renewed hostilities by the Apaches did benefit the O'odham in one way: it discouraged new settlers. But this reprieve was only temporary. Between Mexico's independence and the resumption of Apache raids, large numbers of settlers had moved into the O'odham lands. The settlers sought the good lands of the missions and also began usurping title to the Indians' lands on or near the missions.

Like the old mission lands, boundaries were often not well defined and were difficult to prove legally. Indians also had to fight the settlers over water sources because the land was useless to those who did not control enough water. However, the natives did not know how to use the legal system, and they usually lost their traditional lands.

As the Europeans and their followers moved in, they pushed the O'odham more definitively into the desert. Some O'odham remained in the San Xavier del Bac area, and others moved there when the presidio of Tubac closed due to Apache raids, but Tucson became a town of mixed cultures in which the O'odham played a minor role.

The presidio brought Europeans, European-trained personnel, and then Mexicans. Yaquis moved into the area after Mexican independence, when problems retaining their own native lands in southern Sonora forced many of them to leave. Apaches also settled in the Tucson area during the pacification program. When they promised to remain peaceful, they received lands from the government near what is now called "A" Mountain.

The O'odham were not the only ones affected by increased migration. During the 1830s, the Mexican government had allowed U.S. citizens to move into Texas, and they even encouraged them to do so if they promised to meet certain conditions involving religion and slavery. The flood of migrants eventually created conditions that led, in turn, to the war with Mexico that established the independent Republic of Texas in 1836.

Congress at first refused to annex Texas, although many people in Texas and in the United States desired annexation. In March 1845, however, in his last hours as president, President Tyler signed a joint resolution from the House of Representatives and the Senate that added Texas to the United States. For the O'odham, this was an important step that would lead to the splitting of their lands between two nations. The actions of the United States, which seemed determined to continue expanding, were very disturbing to Mexico.

Trappers from the United States had been using lands as far south as the Gila River since the 1820s. In 1826, Sylvester Pattie and his son, James Ohio, were with a party led by Michel Robidoux that caught numerous beavers along that river and its tributaries. They also engaged in working some abandoned copper mines, which the Apaches allowed because they were not Mexicans.

These were among the first U.S. citizens to reach O'odham territory. James Ohio Pattie credits an Indian attack on the Robidoux party to Papago Indians, but the location on the Gila River indicates that it was probably Apaches. The trappers would not have been interested in O'odham lands because there were no rivers with beavers.

Although Mexican officials objected to violations of their lands, explorers and military parties were active in the northern territories during the 1820s and 1830s. The government had no means to curtail them, and even though Mexican law required trappers to pay a duty on pelts, they seldom paid the government anything.

Within thirty years of the first intrusions by U.S. citizens, many of the O'odham would find themselves under a new government. In May

1846, President Polk manipulated the Congress of the United States into declaring war on Mexico, and less than two years later, the Treaty of Guadalupe Hidalgo ended that war. In twelve years, beginning with the Texas war of independence, Mexico lost more than half of its land to the United States.

The northern provinces were gone or truncated, and still the expansionists in the United States were not satisfied. Mexico's northern border was no more secure than it had been before the war. The presidios were undermanned, and soldiers were leaving daily to hunt for gold. The area was thinly settled and had been further depopulated because of Apache attacks or fear of such attacks. Then Sonora's northern border, which had been the Gila River, was moved farther south because the Treaty of Guadalupe Hidalgo had not included the best route for a transcontinental railroad.

In 1853, President Pierce of the United States sent General James Gadsden to Mexico to negotiate for the purchase of Mexican territory. He was also to negotiate to have the United States relieved of some of the responsibilities accepted in the Treaty of Guadalupe Hidalgo, including maintaining peace along the border and paying Mexico for damages caused by Indian raiders.

Gadsden was to try to purchase as much land as possible for up to $50 million. Santa Anna, the president of Mexico, knew the financial situation of his administration and of the country was desperate, so he decided to sell some land for $10 million. However, even the desperate need for money could not compel him to sell more. The people of the country would not allow it. Nearly all the land sold was in Sonora, and the new boundary divided in two the lands of the O'odham.

In 1854, the U.S. Senate ratified the treaty and established the current international boundary. Mexico thus averted a second war with the United States, which many Mexicans feared, but otherwise, Mexico got little from the treaty. The money Mexico received was not enough to solve its many problems.

Although the United States shouldered the responsibility for Indian raids south of the border, the $10 million that Mexico received for land sold to the United States may not have been equal to Mexico's claims for damages caused by Apaches. The United States had assumed responsibility for the costs of those raids in the Treaty of Guadalupe Hidalgo.

The splitting of O'odham lands between two countries inconvenienced the O'odham somewhat, but it would be many years before

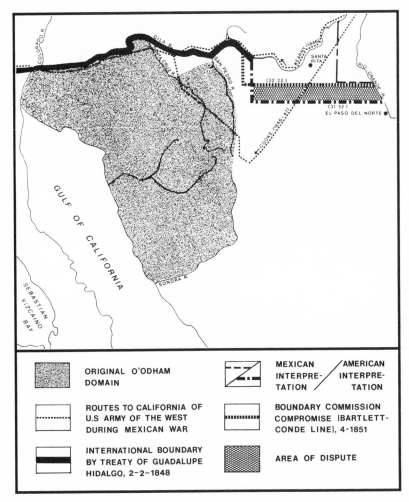

**United States intrusion on O'odham lands**

strong enforcement of border policies would occur. Probably fewer than a thousand O'odham lived south of the boundary created by the treaty, and many of them began moving north as more Mexicans moved onto the best lands along the Altar River.

Otherwise, life for the O'odham continued much as it had. A new government meant little to them. Even though the United States sent troops to suppress the Apaches, it took several years for the army to

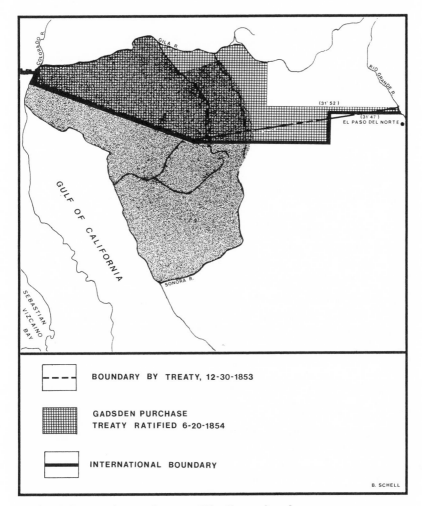

BOUNDARY BY TREATY, 12-30-1853

GADSDEN PURCHASE
TREATY RATIFIED 6-20-1854

INTERNATIONAL BOUNDARY

B. SCHELL

## United States intrusion on O'odham lands

figure out an effective way to slow them down. By then, the Civil War had begun, and the U.S. government recalled the troops. This not only allowed the Apaches to resume and increase their raids but also led them to believe they had forced the army to leave, and they became even more aggressive.

The O'odham went through these difficult times relatively unaffected. They were not involved in the wars for independence, nor did they usually get involved in the subsequent civil wars in Sonora between the followers of Gándara and those of Urrea or Pesqueira, who were the political rivals striving for power in that state. Gándara did solicit Indian aid in an 1838 revolt by promising to help the various Indian tribes retain their lands, but the revolt ended in 1840 when the government deployed troops to establish peace.

For the most part, the O'odham remained at peace with whatever government they had to deal with. Some individuals did become mercenary soldiers with one or another of the political factions fighting periodically in Sonora during this era, but their grounds for this activity was the pay they received rather than political advantage or ideology.

A bigger problem for the O'odham than the political turmoil was increased mining. Most of the mining discoveries in the 1830s were in the Altar district. Miners built gold placers at Quitovac, and Altar became a bustling little town, with a population of 4,000. The town was formerly on the edge of Apache raiding routes but became a major target as it gained wealth. Along with the Apache raids, a small Papago uprising in 1841 caused mines to be abandoned and stock raising and agriculture to be crippled. Altar lost about half of its newly gained population. Then, in 1850, cholera swept through Sonora, and Altar lost more than 1,100 people. How the epidemic affected the O'odham is unknown.

During the 1850s, several filibustering expeditions invaded Sonora. Filibustering expeditions were raids involving citizens of the United States or of France who thought that Sonora would be easy to conquer and separate from Mexico. They thought that the country could be ruled independently or eventually joined to France or the United States. The O'odham were not involved in these raids other than to witness occasional groups of armed men traveling through their lands. Then the O'odham could watch as the infiltrators were hanged for their failed efforts, as was the case with the Crabb expedition of 1857. There was not much good to be learned from these intruders.

In the 1850s, after the Gadsden Purchase gained the area for the United States, prospectors began developing the mines surrounding Tubac. There was relative peace with the Apaches because the Apaches allowed U.S. citizens to work the mines if they left the Apaches alone to do their will in Mexico or paid them for not attacking the miners.

By the end of the Mexican-American War, O'odham lands were bordered by the Anglo-American culture on the north and northeast, and by the Spanish-American culture on the south and southeast. The western O'odham lands faced the Gulf of California, and the ships of both those cultures sailed those waters.

As these intruders continued to draw closer and find more and more uses for the lands that the O'odham had used for centuries as their own, it would be difficult for the O'odham to maintain traditional customs and lifeways.

# 6

## The More Things Change. . . .

*She claimed that we were different. My great-grandmother refused to eat with silverware on the table. She had her nails real long and just cut flat. She used just three fingers to eat with, just like a spoon. She broke her food and picked it up. . . . She would make fun of us. She said, "You mean to tell me you have to wash each and every one of those —." (She wouldn't say "spoons.") And I said, "Yes." She said, "You don't need to do that. Eat like me and you won't have to."*

CLARA BONNIE PRICE, Interview

When the Anglo-Americans came on the scene after victory in the Mexican-American War and completion of the Gadsden Purchase in 1854, a new culture and concept of civilization entered the lands of the O'odham. The Anglo-Americans tried to isolate the native people rather than force their ideas of civilization onto them. To do this, they established reservations, herded the native peoples onto those reservations, and told them to stay there. The more hostile Indians had top priority in placement on reserves, and they received various types of aid to keep them from disturbing the encroaching settlers. This aid usually consisted of food, tools, clothing, and sometimes housing allowances.

Of course, the Anglo-Americans considered themselves carriers of civilization, but there was no urgency about spreading it. They expected native people to observe and gradually adopt the civilization that the Anglos brought. Their concept of civilization included the English language as spoken in the United States, individual title to landholdings, agricultural techniques practiced by U.S. citizens, and the Christian religion, usually any one of the more popular Protestant groups.

Many U.S. citizens believed that it was their destiny to expand their country to natural borders on the North American continent. This concept, called Manifest Destiny, eventually included the idea that the United States was to take its form of government to the people of the world. Part of advanced civilization, U.S. citizens thought, was a democratically elected representative government; however, they did not push this form of government on the native peoples immediately.

The lack of political order within tribes often frustrated the U.S. authorities, who thought that the native people needed some form of authoritarian system with which the government could deal. Therefore, government representatives in many places appointed tribal leaders during this early period, which marked the beginning of tribal-wide government.

In 1865, the government agents dealing with the O'odham selected Many Skirts as the head chief of the tribe. He may have been the most important leader at San Xavier, but he would not have been recognized as a leader by other groups. Those O'odham living west of San Xavier still lived in small, independent groups and had their own leaders.

Although the governments that were instituted were foreign to the tribes, they had to use such governments to deal with the United States, and the O'odham were among those tribes that eventually developed tribal governments for that reason.

Representatives of the U.S. government went to various Indian tribes to establish treaties, and they may have negotiated agreements with Indian tribes in good faith. But the government did not have the will and, perhaps, the power to enforce the treaties. Anglo-American settlers moved onto Indian lands and disregarded all rights of the native peoples as well as the treaties signed by their government.

As mentioned in the previous chapter, after Gadsden purchased the northern part of the Papaguería for the United States, the O'odham were split between two countries. The United States took about two-thirds of the area still inhabited by the O'odham, while the other third remained under Mexico's control. No one asked the O'odham where they would like to be, and no one informed them that their government had changed. Mexican nationals could choose between staying in the United States or returning to Mexican territory. Where other Mexican citizens were located within the O'odham lands, information about the change in government was available, but some O'odham still maintained allegiance to Mexico decades later because no one had told them about the new international boundary. Regardless of the change, their lives had not been altered.

The treaties with Mexico of 1848 and 1853 that transferred control of O'odham lands from Mexico to the United States clearly protected the rights to the land of those Mexican citizens who chose to remain in the ceded territory. The O'odham under Mexican jurisdiction had full rights to Mexican citizenship, so under provisions of the treaties, their rights to the land remained unrestricted. Their rights to freedom of religion and ownership of their sacred places also remained legally unchanged as they were assimilated into the United States, where they were to have all the constitutional guarantees afforded by that nation to any of its citizens.

In practice, however, the O'odham had few or no rights as the intruding Anglos took what they wanted and ignored the rights of native peoples. In the United States, as had happened earlier in Mexico, the Indians could not prove ownership by means of legal documentation. Because Indians usually did not consider land as an item of individual possession, they had little need to document ownership. To the intruding settlers, any land that the government had not reserved for exclusive use by Indians was considered part of the public domain. This made the lands open for settling or claiming in the eyes of the in-migrating hordes of Anglo-Americans.

The Tohono O'odham were seldom aggressive or hostile towards the settlers. Not only were the O'odham peaceful, they were allies of the United States and the settlers in their conflicts with the Apaches. The U.S. government did not have to send troops against the O'odham to protect either the settlers or its interests, and consequently, the federal government basically ignored the O'odham and their rights.

The U.S. government recognized the O'odham as an independent tribe from the beginning, but it made no effort to establish a reservation for them because they were peaceful. In 1857, the government sent agent John Walker to deal with the Papagos, as the O'odham were known then. The government clearly distinguished them from the Gila River Pimas who spoke a dialect of the same language. The agent, stationed in Tucson, dealt with the O'odham in that town and at San Xavier, and he distributed agricultural hand tools, knives, cooking implements, and flour among them. He did not understand the means of desert survival that the O'odham had developed through many years, and he thought they were starving.

Although the government recognized the O'odham to the west in what is now the main reservation area, the government knew little about them. For the most part, all the government did about the O'odham in outlying areas was estimate how many were there. Agents made various population estimates in the early years of U.S. control, ranging from 3,670 in 1861, to 6,800 in 1863. Charles D. Poston based his estimate of 6,800 on his counting of O'odham located in eighteen villages in the area west and south of Tucson.

The O'odham caused the U.S. government almost no problems because they were industrious and peaceful, but their reward was to be treated as if they did not exist. The government simply neglected them and their rights to their lands while cattlemen and miners used those lands for their own purposes and drove the O'odham from water sources that their ancestors had used for centuries.

The constant migration of non-Indians into the region was the gravest threat to the O'odham. At first, the Apaches had kept out all but a small number of miners and drifters. Many of these people had given up on the California goldfields and were looking for new areas to prospect. Others were returning home, but decided to stay in the Tucson area for various reasons. Then, as the U.S. government sent dragoons to occupy the presidios abandoned by the Mexicans, more and more farmers and ranchers began claiming land.

Further complicating the land issue was the fact that the Tohono O'odham did not use the same land or fields all year. Their pattern of migrating to the mountains during the dry season and returning to their fields when it rained meant that during much of the year, one or both villages would be unoccupied. Also, gathering food from the desert required that they move for shorter periods to areas where those matured foods could be harvested.

The O'odham did not build permanent structures in either of the primary villages, and cattlemen or others would enter an area, find no one around, and assume that no one lived there. The O'odham would return later to find that these intruders had taken their lands, but they had little say in the matter because they did not know how to use the legal system that the invading people brought (and sometimes respected). Without that knowledge, the O'odham could not use the system for their protection.

In 1862, the United States made the public lands of southern Arizona Territory available to homesteaders, and in 1866, an act of Congress opened the lands, except those covered by claims based upon Spanish or Mexican law, to mineral entry. This subjected O'odham lands more than before to the intrusion of miners, cattlemen, and homesteaders.

By the mid-1860s, the O'odham near Tucson were feeling the pressures of encroachment, and they asked that their ancient land be marked and that it be respected by Anglo-Americans and Mexicans. They requested at least the same recognition of their lands as that given by the Spanish and Mexican governments.

The agents assigned to the Papagos pushed for a reservation at San Xavier, but they could not agree whether all the O'odham should be brought there, or whether a reservation should be made to the west, where the government would have to dig wells to provide a permanent residence for them. During this time, the O'odham living near Tucson or at San Xavier received the tribe's allocations of provisions and tools, while the majority were more or less ignored, except for the occasional visit from a government census taker.

In 1874, an executive order established the reservation at San Xavier and set aside 69,200 acres surrounding the mission for the use of the O'odham. A school, already established at the mission for the O'odham children, enrolled and taught eighty-nine students. The following year, the Pima agency in Sacaton took over the affairs of the Tohono O'odham, and the San Xavier school was discontinued in favor of the school at Sacaton.

After the U.S. government created the San Xavier Reservation, the O'odham continually complained that Mexicans were living there, using the water, grazing cattle, and farming the land. The agents also noted that the Mexicans were cutting the mesquite trees of the reservation and selling the wood in Tucson. Non-Indians cut most of the trees on the reservation, and the O'odham received nothing.

In 1884, an executive order created a small reservation for O'odham who had moved north to the Gila River, west of the Pima lands. The Gila Bend Reservation, as it was called, was not large, and later it was made smaller to accommodate the demands of encroaching whites who wanted the land and the water that was available there.

Although only about 10 percent of the O'odham lived on the two small reservations, all of them had to learn how to deal effectively with the new political authority and the reality of the intruding culture. It would take time to gain formal recognition and protection of their land, but when they finally achieved that goal, it was partly a result of what the O'odham learned through the experiences with these two early reservations.

The Gadsden treaty of 1854 stipulated that the United States would control the Apaches and keep them from attacking Mexico, but after the Mexican army pulled out of Tucson, it was years before the United States sent replacements. In the meantime, the miners who

Mother and child on the reservation (Courtesy of Venito Garcia
Library, Sells)

moved into the region used two approaches to avoid Apache raids.
One method was to make individual treaties and buy freedom from
attack. The other was to form a private militia and ally with the O'odham for mutual protection.

Both the O'odham and the settlers benefited from keeping the
Apaches away, but the Mexicans continued to suffer. Even after the
U.S. troops arrived, there were not enough to control the Apaches, so
some settlers and miners continued buying peace by personal arrange-
ment. Even the troops occasionally bought themselves peace and allowed the Apaches to do as they wanted south of the border.

None of these methods proved totally effective, and the O'odham
still feared raids by the Apaches. Sometimes the Apaches abducted
women and children and sold these captives as slaves to other Indians,
or forced them to work for the Apaches themselves. The O'odham
told many stories about the abductions and escapes of those kid-
napped. Because capture after an attempted escape could mean death,
it took resourcefulness and clever preparations to escape the Apaches
and travel alone back to the homeland.

Many captives were treated well, however, and often were adopted
into Apache groups. After peace treaties between the O'odham and

the Apaches became final, many captives had the choice to remain with the Apaches or return to their homeland. Because many were married and had families, a large number of them chose to stay.

Even though Apaches had forced the O'odham to abandon villages east of the Santa Cruz Valley, the O'odham continued to use the lands, but in a limited way. Threat of attack kept them very wary during these forays, but hunters still pursued game in the traditional land, and groups went to the traditional gathering places to find foods in season. In 1852, observers saw O'odham in temporary camps on the east slopes of the Santa Rita Mountains near the San Pedro River. They continued to gather agaves in that region, but permanent settlement of the area remained impractical.

To help keep the Apaches in check, the U.S. Army recruited Papago and Pima warriors, who served as scouts and as troops when needed. The short period between the arrival of U.S. troops and the beginning of the Civil War afforded some protection for both non-Indians and the O'odham; however, the Civil War, which began in 1861, adversely affected the security of the O'odham. The government withdrew most federal troops, and the only action that the remaining troops had was against each other as regional loyalties divided federal forces. Troops from Texas initially prevailed in what is now Arizona, but a company of California volunteers soon took control of the territory.

Most of the Indians certainly did not care one way or the other, but the Apaches believed that they were responsible for the troops leaving, and they became more aggressive. The result was that the O'odham faced increased threats from the Apaches, who now had free rein over the territory.

Renewed attacks forced the O'odham to move back into the defensive villages, which they had been leaving during the period of lesser tensions, and as they gathered in larger villages, it was necessary to have more powerful leaders. The O'odham still grouped themselves with others who spoke similar dialects, and leaders within these groups organized defensive actions.

Defense was probably the only reason leadership powers extended beyond the villages within the O'odham system; traditional government consisted of a village council of elders that made most of the decisions for the local group. In order to provide adequate defense, however, leaders had to make important decisions involving several villages without consulting the councils of elders.

Raiding by the Apaches extended beyond the Civil War as they took advantage of the lack of a strong military presence and began to raid the increasing numbers of settlers who arrived after the Civil War ended in 1865. Although the United States had experienced soldiers to protect the interests of the nation, it took years to eliminate the threat of Apache attack and bring peace to the new settlers, the O'odham, and the Mexicans.

One incident that led to treaty negotiations occurred in 1871. Cattle were a magnet to the Apaches, and in 1871, a group of them made a foray to San Xavier and drove off a number of cattle and horses. The community leaders at Tucson then approached Francisco, the O'odham head chief of the area, and asked for help in organizing a posse. The posse eventually consisted of six Americans, forty-eight Mexicans, and ninety-four O'odham.

This group made a rapid march by night to Camp Grant, about sixty miles northeast of Tucson in the San Pedro Valley. Not far from Camp Grant was a village of Apaches who had come there to receive promised rations from the government. Those who lived there were supposed to give up raiding and stealing, but some of the San Xavier and Tucson residents insisted that the tracks of the raiders who stole their herds led to that settlement.

In a surprise attack, the posse killed a large number of the Apaches. The army commander at Camp Grant reported that the posse killed 21 women and children, but other reports indicate that as many as 125 people died in the raid. The victors took nearly 30 Apache children to Mexico and sold them as slaves. Of those abducted and sold, only 6 children eventually returned.

After the Camp Grant massacre, the Apaches began to look for peace between themselves and the O'odham, and a treaty in 1872 signified an attempt to improve relations among the various tribes of the Southwest. The treaty was celebrated as complete on May 20, 1872, by representatives of the Mexicans, Americans, Pimas, O'odham, Maricopas, and Apaches from southern Arizona, who all signed the treaty. However, even though conditions improved, it was three years before Apaches stopped raiding the O'odham. When peace returned, the O'odham could again spread out into the small villages they preferred.

As ranches developed in the Santa Cruz Valley, animals were tempting targets for those who could rustle a few horses or cows and head quickly for the border to sell them in Mexico. If the rustlers could drive the captured cattle over the border without being caught, they could make a nice profit, and the O'odham were involved occasionally in such theft.

By the late 1860s, cattle ranching had become big business in the O'odham lands. The Santa Cruz Valley south of San Xavier became a major stock-raising area, and Anglo-Americans brought large herds from Texas. Mexicans brought smaller herds from Mexico to graze there. In 1869, a man named Hooker took a herd of cattle to the Baboquivari range and left them with the O'odham to tend. Earlier he had kept a herd in a valley east of the mountains, and he had lost about four hundred head to the O'odham, but he thought that was just compensation for being able to raise his animals there.

In 1871, the agent reported that the O'odham in the west had herds of stock, and the possession of stock indicated that traditional life was beginning to change considerably. Stock raising was a custom that the O'odham had borrowed slowly from the intruders, but members of villages around the Baboquivari Mountains were undoubtedly influenced by encroaching cattlemen and the groups that had come north from Mexico. Farther west, the effect was not as noticeable because the O'odham who lived there did not have the same intensive contact with cattle ranching, and their lands were not as suitable for grazing.

Some O'odham also began working in the mines. Mining activity had increased between the completion of the Gadsden Purchase and the Civil War of the United States, and many who had failed to strike gold in California turned their attention to Arizona. The miners again worked the areas that had been mined occasionally in the Santa Cruz River drainage, and they also established new mines, giving the O'odham on the eastern fringes of their lands an opportunity to work for wages. By 1858, they had begun to reestablish villages there. Some O'odham also found work in Tucson, doing whatever labor was required. During this period, the O'odham who had the most contact with the Anglos began to be immersed in the newcomers' cash economy.

In northern Sonora, there had been a minor economic boom when miners began working in the Gadsden Purchase area. Some of the Hispanics who had been driven out of the region by the Apaches returned when the Anglo-Americans negotiated or purchased a kind of peace.

In the 1850s, men successfully worked the copper mine at Ajo; however, it was such a long distance across a waterless desert to a railroad that could transport ore that the mine did not remain profitable. Miners also operated the silver mines near Tubac with some profit, but after the Civil War began, hostile Apaches made continued operation impractical. This resumption of Apache raids reduced mining activity considerably, and it was slow to recover afterwards. One reason for the slow recovery after the war was that investment capital from the United States went to the Rocky Mountain region rather than to the Southwest. Major mineral deposits newly discovered in Colorado attracted miners and men willing to invest in the development of those mines.

Mining in the Southwest increased again in the 1870s. Some miners successfully reopened the Ajo mine, and others worked small claims throughout the O'odham lands, particularly in the Comobabi Mountains. A successful claim would cause a flurry of activity, and sometimes O'odham workers found employment at the mining camps. After the miners exhausted the ore and moved on, the O'odham would move into the area to take advantage of wells that the miners had dug.

Although they were slow to embrace a cash economy, the O'odham had exhibited some commercial enterprise in the early period when they came under the jurisdiction of the United States. The first Indian agent assigned to them reported that they supplied Tucson, Tubac, and some mines with salt from a salt lake near the coast. The salt pilgrimage, which had been a tradition of the O'odham, led to a means of earning money as they began to adjust to the ways of the overbearing and ever-encroaching culture.

The miners also needed food, and they provided a new and expanding market for produce, which led to increased cultivation in the Altar and Magdalena valleys. This, in turn, increased the demand for labor and brought more people into the region. The O'odham south of the border were affected both positively and negatively; on one hand, they were able to secure employment on the farms, but the increased land use drove many of them away from what remained of their traditional lands.

After the Civil War, more Anglo-American settlers began moving into Arizona. For the most part, they settled along the river bottoms where water was available and the land was better suited for farming. Unfortunately for the Pimas, the settlers diverted waters upstream of their lands, and soon not enough water flowed downstream to maintain the Pima agriculture. The O'odham at San Xavier and Gila Bend experienced similar problems.

The new farmers soon began producing enough food to sell to the miners, and that put an end to the prosperity of the Altar and Magdalena areas. As a result, the O'odham found fewer opportunities for work in Mexico, but they began to find more work at higher wages in Arizona and California. Also, the political turmoil in Sonora contrasted markedly with the relative calm in Arizona, and the Apaches continued to raid more often in Mexico than in Arizona. Many of the O'odham found these conditions to be incentives to move northward, leaving even fewer of them in the Mexican part of the O'odham lands.

Another reason the O'odham began to move northward was that the Hispanics in Mexico had no more regard for their rights to their lands than the Anglo-Americans in the United States. In fact, Hispanics and O'odham fought battles over water in the Mexican area much more often than they did north of the border, where they could live more easily in their traditional manner.

The O'odham who remained in Mexico were more likely to be assimilated into Mexican society than were those in the United States to be incorporated in the Anglo-American culture. The Mexicans accepted Indians more readily than most U.S. citizens, but this acceptance led to the Indians abandoning traditional lifeways and joining the dominant culture. For the O'odham who wished to continue traditional ways, life was as difficult in Mexico as it was north of the border. It took many years before the Mexican government began to recognize the special need for land for the O'odham.

The O'odham in Mexico still occasionally became involved in the partisan politics of the Sonoran state. During the U.S. Civil War, France had become involved in Mexican politics, and parties supporting the French interests had become strong in Sonora. They were never as successful there as they were in Chihuahua, but there was considerable infighting to bring the French supporters into power. When partisans recruited the native Indian peoples to aid the French side, some of the O'odham joined with them.

After the Civil War ended, however, the United States decided to invoke the Monroe Doctrine and eliminate meddling by the French in Mexican politics. With the United States supporting an independent Mexico with the most powerful and experienced army in the world, the French decided to abandon all attempts to gain a foothold in Mexico. In Sonora, the conservative factions then prevailed, and conditions did not change much for the O'odham.

Along with the cultural pressures resulting from changes in governments and increased numbers of settlers in and surrounding O'odham lands, the Catholic church continued to exert its influence. There is little information about church activities between the dissolution of the missions in the 1830s and the first decade of the twentieth century, when some priests were active among the O'odham, but obviously the influence of the church continued. Even O'odham who lived far from the major population centers seem to have been baptized and to have recognized their membership in the church.

Most O'odham who accepted the Christian religion, however, were involved with Sonoran Catholicism, an unofficial branch of the Catholic church that developed after the missionaries had left the region. Sonoran Catholicism was adapted to the needs of the various groups in Sonora and included elements of both native religion and Catholicism, but rejected the authority of church-trained priests. Participants in Sonoran Catholicism built most of the small chapels that still grace the villages of the O'odham lands, where they continue to celebrate significant religious holidays.

Of all the O'odham, the Hia C'ed O'odham suffered the greatest changes during the 1850s and 1860s. An epidemic of some kind killed most of them in the 1850s; it has been estimated that only four families survived. Then the miners at Ajo and the ranchers at Quitobaquito took some of their most desirable land. The Hia C'ed O'odham managed to survive, and some found employment constructing the railroad through the Gila River basin. They remained scattered and never completely assimilated into the main body of O'odham.

After Mexicans accused the southern Hia C'ed O'odham of attacking migrants traveling to California by way of the Camino del Diablo, the Mexican army gathered most of them and removed them from the western end of O'odham lands. On the basis of the accusation, which no one bothered to prove, the Mexican officials justified their actions against those defenseless people, and the army relocated them to Quitovac and other areas inland, where they joined other O'odham.

The period between the end of the Mexican-American War and the U.S. Civil War marked the beginning of many changes, including splitting the O'odham between two countries, but for most O'odham, conditions did not change markedly. Eventually, though, considerable differences between the two countries resulted in differing opportunities for the O'odham of each region.

The middle of the nineteenth century was a distinct turning point for the O'odham. They willingly changed some things and slowly and reluctantly changed others. Some of them in close proximity to towns began to accept a cash economy to sustain life. The future years would be a struggle to adapt as pressure on their culture continued unabated.

# 7

## Workin' on the Railroad and Elsewhere

*. . . Things like corn and squash and watermelon and things like that.*
*And when they harvested their crop, they gave it out to their relatives,*
*and when they did the planting, they did it together.*

ASCENSION ANTON, Interview

During the last quarter of the nineteenth century and the early years of
the twentieth, the O'odham began to move slowly away from their
traditional way of life. Their land and its uses began to change. Some
O'odham began to attend schools, while others began to rely upon
wage work as an important source of livelihood. Some even became
involved in commercial cattle raising on a limited scale.

Though the U.S. government established reservations for the O'odham in 1874 and 1882, it paid little attention to the needs of the people. Most O'odham stayed outside the reservations, and the government all but ignored them until the turn of the century. Even those
living at the San Xavier or Gila Bend reservations received little con-
sideration because the government agency that administered O'odham lands was not on either one. The agency was located at Sacaton
and was also the headquarters of the Gila River Pima and the Salt
River Maricopa reservations.

This government agency was supposed to watch over and protect
O'odham lands, but because the agency was geographically separated
from the reservation, it was not able to maintain adequate surveillance.
One major problem was the number of Mexican Americans who
moved onto the reservation land. The reservations were attractive to
squatters (people who moved onto the land without legal ownership)
because the land was good, and water accessible. Finally, in 1882,
with the assistance of the Indian agent, the O'odham at San Xavier
expelled most of the non-Indians who had trespassed on their lands.

Only one group of non-Indians remained on the reservation: the
refugees from Tubac who had fled their homeland to avoid Apache
attacks. In 1848, a law passed in Sonora had given them ownership

rights to vacant or uncultivated lands near San Xavier or Tucson. One of the refugees, José María Martínez, had applied for a tract of land at San Xavier. After Mexican authorities discussed the matter with the local O'odham, they gave Martínez permission to settle there and pasture his cattle on the community's common grounds. This created the Martinez Land Grant, which allowed the heirs of Martínez to claim some of the O'odham lands; under the provisions of the Gadsden Purchase, the United States agreed to honor land grants within the former Mexican territory.

In 1884, the same agent who had helped evict squatters two years earlier decided to remove the Martínez heirs living on the reservation. He reasoned that since the United States had not verified the land grant when it purchased the land from Mexico, the Martínez family had no right to remain on the reservation. María Martínez de Smith, one of the daughters of José María Martínez, had married John M. Berger, a jeweler from Tucson, and they ran the ranch on the reservation. After the agent evicted the Bergers, their house was vandalized, perhaps by the agent's assistants. The Bergers sued in U.S. courts to have their land rights restored, and they eventually won the suit and received title to seventy acres of land. In August 1887, they returned to the ranch. The government purchased thirty acres of this land for the San Xavier Reservation in 1916, but the remaining forty acres stayed under private ownership.

Three years after his return, Berger became the farmer-in-charge on the reservation. He was the first government administrator to be in residence since 1876, when the agency moved to Sacaton. Berger later became the Indian agent for the San Xavier Reservation and served in this office until 1910.

The same year that the U.S. government evicted Mexican American squatters from O'odham lands, it granted two railroad companies rights of way through the reservation. Southern Arizona Railroad received permission to run a route south from Tucson to the Mexican border, and in return, the company was to build a schoolhouse for the O'odham on the San Xavier Reservation. The company built neither the railroad nor the schoolhouse. Another railroad company proposed a route that would run west to serve the mines in what is now the main reservation of the O'odham, and then continue on to the Pacific coast. This proposal did not go beyond the planning stage.

The Southern Pacific Railroad had already completed a route to the Pacific along the Gila River in 1879. The railroad passed through the

BUREAU OF AMERICAN ETHNOLOGY, NO.    WILLIAM DINWIDDIE, PHOTOGRAPHER.

J. M. Berger, farmer-in-charge, San Xavier Indian Reservation, *center; fifth from left,* Carlos Rios; *next left,* Francisco Rios; *next left,* Jose Juan Cristobal; *tenth from left,* Jose Lewis; *next left, seated on ground,* Ok-sa-ga-wa; *next left, against wall,* Juan Capon; *first from right,* Octaviano Nuñez. Group gathered to discuss plans for Feast of St. Francis Xavier. (Dinwiddie photograph, 1894, courtesy of Special Collections, University of Arizona Library)

area of Gila Bend, where for as long as is known, the O'odham from Chuilikam had gathered food and sometimes planted crops. It apparently was never a permanent settlement, but when the railroad was being built, many O'odham moved to Gila Bend and remained there while the men worked on construction of the railroad bed. Some of them stayed after completion of the railroad, and in 1882, by executive order, President Chester A. Arthur created a reservation to protect O'odham settlements and land rights at Gila Bend.

From its outset, the Gila Bend Reservation was beset by conflicts with Anglo-American settlers over water rights and canal building. The new settlers took most of the water, and then in 1889, Congress authorized construction of a new canal across the reservation, with the requirement that the O'odham would be supplied with the water

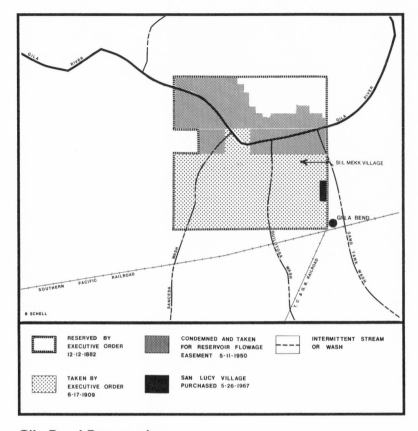

## Gila Bend Reservation

they needed free of charge. Once the settlers completed the canal, more non-Indians came into the area and made demands on the water and lands that the O'odham used.

Another conflict was caused by O'odham grazing practices. The O'odham allowed their horses and cattle to roam freely over lands they held in common. Because there were no adequate fences, however, these animals also entered adjoining lands, where they damaged the ditch banks, fields, and gardens of non-Indians. The non-Indians would then capture O'odham livestock and turn them over to the deputy sheriff. When the sheriff did not return their animals, the O'odham would raid the deputy, rescue their animals, and flee south.

These conflicts over grazing and water rights caused much unrest in the area, and this led the Arizona delegation to find a congressman to propose a bill to move the O'odham of Gila Bend to San Xavier. The bill, introduced early in 1890, was favored by the administration and most of the influential people in Arizona, but it met defeat because many congressmen felt that it would be unfair to the O'odham.

Conditions at Gila Bend did not improve, however, and as non-Indians established more farms upstream on the Gila River, the reservation's water supply continued to diminish. Then, in 1909, President Taft restored more than half of the Gila Bend Reservation to the public domain, including Si:l Mekk, the main village of the O'odham. Having lost their favored homesites, more and more O'odham left the area, and the reservation of 10,297 remaining acres became nearly deserted.

Ongoing problems and costs involved in maintaining the reservations led to major changes in the government's policies toward all Indian people. Reservations became attractive places to the Anglo immigrants because earlier immigrants had already claimed the more attractive, fertile lands. In order to reduce the cost of reservations and also to provide more lands for settlers, Congress passed the Dawes Act, or General Allotment Act, in February 1887. Through the influence of the Bureau of Indian Affairs, the federal government had decided that the best way to make Indians behave like the majority of its citizens was to force them to change the way they thought about the land.

Unlike Anglos, the Indians of most tribes in the United States never believed that individuals could own land. Instead, land was something that the members of a tribe valued, shared, and protected for their community and for future generations.

Although each O'odham family could have land upon which they lived and worked, they did not think of it as personal property. If a family abandoned a particular tract of land, another family could occupy and use that land without recompense. This allowed the O'odham to move about freely and find the best lands for planting crops and gathering food. Each family found its own land and worked as much as it could. When the size of a family changed, so did the size of that family's fields.

The government did not understand the Indian concept of mutually owned land, and it decided that all reservation lands should be broken up into small, privately owned allotments, with each Indian owning his or her own private plot. After each Indian received an allotment, whatever reservation land remained would be opened for purchase and settlement by Anglos. In this way, the government reasoned, the Indians would eventually adopt the way of life and farming techniques of their Anglo neighbors.

The allotment of O'odham land did not begin until 1890. It started at San Xavier because the agent for the O'odham and the Pima believed that this was one of the few places in the Southwest deserts where a 160-acre allotment was large enough to supply sufficient food for a family. The agent counted 363 O'odham at San Xavier and considered all of them residents. Some of them were descendants of the Sobaipuris who had lived in the San Xavier region for centuries. Others were only visitors, but they received parcels of land, too. However, residents of San Xavier who happened to be away at the time missed out on the allotments.

When the allotments were complete, ninety-four heads of families had received 160 acres each. A single allotment included 20 acres of farmland and 50 to 80 acres of mesquite timberland. The rest of the allotment was mesa land, useful only for grazing. Married women received no land of their own but were expected to share their husbands' allotments. All single persons, both female and male, received a 40- or 80-acre parcel of mesa land. In total, the U.S. government allotted nearly 42,000 of the 71,090 acres of San Xavier lands.

Even though the reservation was divided into individually owned allotments, the O'odham continued to work the land as they had for many years, ignoring the artificial boundaries imposed by the government. Eventually they began moving to private plots, but they still did not understand the laws governing property ownership. For example, the original owners of allotments seldom made wills, so when they died, land was divided among the heirs, who received equal parcels under Arizona law. In time, ownership of the land at San Xavier became quite fragmented and confusing.

When Congress authorized the division of Indian land under the Dawes Act, the government assumed it would take time for Indians to adjust to Anglo notions of land ownership, so it made provisions to protect the allotments for twenty-five years. The government further assumed that after that much time, the Indians would be able to make more knowledgeable decisions about the use of their privately owned land. After twenty-five years, Indian owners were to receive title to their lands in fee simple, which meant they could do whatever they wanted with their property. They could sell it, or they could pass it on to their heirs.

However, Indians could receive title to their lands before the twenty-five-year period expired if the Indian agent of a reservation declared them knowledgeable enough to handle their own affairs. For example, the agent at San Xavier issued Pedro Eusebio a fee-simple title to his allotment in 1909. Eusebio then sold a forty-acre tract along with a smaller parcel. However, he apparently did not understand what the sale was about. In a hearing called to explain what had happened, Eusebio's son testified that his father, who had since died, did not know the consequences of the action. He did not know that he was signing away rights to his allotment. Nevertheless, for many years, outsiders owned the land that Eusebio had sold.

Near the end of 1894, an executive order gave agents permission to divide the Gila Bend Reservation into allotments, and a proposal submitted by an allotment agent in July 1896 would have divided the reservation into 679 ten-acre plots. The proposal was never approved, however, and as a result, the Gila Bend Reservation remained a commonly owned tract of land.

Most of the O'odham still lived off the reservations, in the vast desert region of southwestern Arizona, but even though the O'odham had inhabited this area for centuries, they had no legal rights to the land. The government considered it part of the public domain.

In 1886, the Indian agent, Roswell Wheeler, tried to persuade the O'odham to gain legal protection for their lands. He surveyed lands in the center of O'odham territory that seemed most favorable for homesteads, and then he encouraged the O'odham to file for titles under federal homestead laws. However, the O'odham saw no need to apply for the land they had always occupied.

Without legal title to this vast territory, the O'odham faced the increasing danger of having their homelands taken over by ranchers. Cattle raising had become profitable in Arizona Territory after the completion of the southern route of the transcontinental railroad system in the early 1880s, and over time, cattlemen moved ever larger herds into the region. They also brought high-quality breeding stock to improve the herds, and as long as freight charges remained low, the railroads could transport cattle profitably to markets in the East or West. Also, the climate during the early 1880s was unusually wet, giving the area an excellent grass cover. Thus conditions for the expansion of the Anglo-owned cattle industry were extremely good.

As their herds grew, the Anglo-American cattlemen moved farther onto the O'odham lands and established ranches without regard for the rights of the O'odham who already lived there. As a result, competition for the scarce grazing land and water resources increased, and in some cases, the intruding cattlemen pushed O'odham cattle owners and farmers away from sites they had maintained and improved for years. Armed with better weapons, the more aggressive and better organized Anglo-American cattlemen were able to intimidate the O'odham. They were also able to use the law to their advantage in taking the lands they wanted.

Despite a growing friction with non-Indian cattle owners, the O'odham continued to raise their own herds. These herds were small and were allowed to roam freely. They were kept primarily for subsistence, and when an O'odham family slaughtered an animal, it shared the meat freely with all the village families. This was the same custom the O'odham ancestors had followed when they killed deer.

As O'odham cattle herds grew and required more range for grazing, families, too, began to spread out and cover more land. No longer afraid of the Apaches, whose attacks had virtually ceased by 1874, the O'odham started to move away from the large villages they had built for defense in an earlier time. Instead of living in or near what may have been as few as eleven large villages, the O'odham families scattered and took up residence in many smaller, widely separated communities.

By the end of the nineteenth century, a few O'odham families at the south end of the Baboquivari Mountains were raising cattle for sale and competing with Anglos for good rangeland. In addition to this competition, other factors made life difficult for the Anglo cattlemen. The region's fragile desert grasslands were becoming overgrazed, and when a drought hit in 1885, many cattle died before they could be rounded up and driven to better ranges. As the amount and quality of the grasslands continued to decline, many Anglo ranchers were forced out of the region, and eventually O'odham cattlemen took over some of the areas left vacant.

As more and more O'odham raised cattle for the marketplace, some of their traditional values began to change. Before this time, the O'odham tradition did not teach that an individual should acquire wealth. Surplus wealth was always redistributed, and the gambling rivalry between villages was one way the O'odham did this. When members of different villages competed with each other, they wagered a good part of their possessions, including cattle and horses. The losses could be immense, but a losing village always worked hard to replace its goods or win them back at another challenge.

After the turn of the century, however, some individuals who owned large herds withdrew from the village contests and betting. Instead of including surplus cattle in a village's wager, they kept the cattle to build larger herds, which they would sell to non-Indians for cash. Shortly after 1900, the traditional intervillage betting ended.

The rangeland was damaged not only because the cattle ate the grass, but also because the cattle fed on mesquite. Because the mesquite seeds are too hard for cattle to digest, they were dropped in well-fertilized bunches throughout the range. This increased the spread of mesquite trees, which hinder the growth of grass, and as the grasses declined, erosion increased. Because the cattlemen, O'odham and Anglo alike, considered the number of their animals more important than the health of the range, much of the fragile desert grassland was unable to heal itself. The damage from overgrazing was too great.

At the same time that Anglo cattlemen were taking over grasslands in the 1870s and 1880s, miners were also seeking riches in the mountains of the O'odham lands. Unlike cattle ranching, mining was not very disruptive to the O'odham way of life. Since most of the mines were in the mountains away from where the O'odham lived and worked, the O'odham did not deal with many miners. Occasionally there were arguments over valuable water or land, but these did not lead to long-lasting rivalries.

Gunsight, Fresnal Lode, Cababi Mines, Quijotoa, Brownell, Prieta, Bahia, and Logan were some of the mines and mining towns established on O'odham lands. Quijotoa was probably the most successful, and at one point in the 1880s, it had about two hundred buildings and perhaps as many as ten thousand non-Indians. However, the town, which consisted of four subdivisions around the old village of Quijotoa, was built more on rumor and speculation than on substantial ore reserves. The ore body that had stimulated the growth of Quijotoa proved to be small and played out rapidly, and within a few years, the town was abandoned.

Most of the other mines, and the towns that the miners built up around them, also were short-lived. Only the large Ajo copper mine, which has been working off and on for more than a century, was large enough to sustain long-term mining.

After the ore was depleted and mining ceased, the O'odham did gain use of whatever the miners had left behind, including buildings and wells. Both were valuable assets but impossible to move, so the O'odham often built new communities around the camps and water resources that the miners had abandoned.

Like cattle ranching, mining had an adverse effect on the O'odham's fragile desert lands. As mesquite and other vegetation were destroyed to supply the mines with timber, and the miners with fuel, the desert lost more of its protection against erosion and destructive flooding. Without leaves to break the fall of the often torrential desert rain, and without roots to hold the soil, water runoff was much more rapid than when the desert had been undisturbed.

In 1894 and 1901, disastrous floods devastated San Xavier. In earlier years, the flooding of the Santa Cruz River had been a normal occurrence, but the water runoff had not been as rapid or destructive. The roots of trees and plants had held the soil in place and allowed much of the flooding water to be slowed and absorbed. Also, the debris carried by floodwaters was then deposited on the ground, which helped to renew the soil and make it more fertile. Once the vegetation was gone, however, there was nothing to slow the water, and it came with such force that it dug deep channels through the desert floors. The floods lowered the channel of the Santa Cruz River by several feet and eroded the banks, widening the channel considerably.

The rushing waters also tore up fields and carried off houses in San Xavier. The waters washed away some of the best soil and destroyed ditches used to irrigate the fields. After the floods, the ditches were useless anyway because the river channel was too low for water to be drawn into the irrigation system. The ditches then had to be extended upriver until, finally, they could not be extended farther because of conflicts with other farmers. Erosion also caused the underground water level to drop, making the shallow wells that the residents of San Xavier had used for centuries useless.

At the turn of the century, there was interest in expanding the land and water resources for the O'odham, and the Indian Bureau proposed creating small reservations around improved water sites in the central area of the Papaguería. The bureau had wells dug at Indian Oasis (which later became Sells) and several other locations, but Congress never officially created the reservations.

With deep wells as a permanent source of water, the O'odham no longer needed to live in small groups or move from place to place. Larger numbers of O'odham were able to congregate around reliable water supplies and remain in one place for the entire year, and this reversed the trend of the O'odham to spread out into smaller villages. When the threat of Apache attacks had vanished and their cattle needed more rangeland, they had moved to the traditional small villages. Once they had permanent, reliable water sources and horses and wagons for transportation, they again began to move back into larger villages.

The economic system of the O'odham also continued to change. When cattle ranching and mining were profitable, some O'odham worked for the Anglos, who often paid them with hard currency. The O'odham used cash to buy tools and clothing, and also food to supplement their crops, especially in years of poor harvests.

The cash economy became increasingly more important each year, and as the O'odham began to depend more on cash earnings from employment, their migratory cycle changed. When the O'odham were not working their fields or harvesting cactus fruit, they often moved temporarily from their homesteads to find wage work. They worked as construction workers on the railways, as cowboys for Anglo ranchers, and as laborers in the mines.

The O'odham also worked as field hands during springtime harvests on farms across the border in Mexico, and the desert O'odham often traveled north to help the Pima harvest their crops. The O'odham did not always receive wages for their work among the Pimas, but they were able to take home part of what they harvested. At this time of year, they also traded with the Pima, bringing cactus jelly, cholla buds, or other native foods in exchange for wheat. An Indian agent at the Pima reservation once noted that the O'odham returned home with only two sacks of wheat loaded on their ponies, and apparently he thought that was very little wheat compared to the amount of work they had done. However, the O'odham had to do whatever was possible to obtain enough food for their families.

Some O'odham even moved to Tucson to find employment, especially during the years when non-Indian cattle ranchers occupied their lands. Many lived on the outskirts of the city. The women worked as domestics, and men found odd jobs involving manual labor, but the work was usually temporary, and the pay poor.

O'odham also traveled to more distant regions to find employment. Some were hired to work on rail lines far away from their homeland, including fifty O'odham workers who went to Los Angeles in 1900. When the Southern Pacific Railroad hired them, the company promised to pay for their return fare but never did. Because they were allowed to ride free on freight cars in Arizona, some of the workers walked to Yuma from Los Angeles to catch a ride back to Tucson or Gila Bend. Others spent much of their savings to buy tickets to Yuma to save themselves the long walk. For them, the time spent working away from their homes proved to be not very profitable.

That same year, other groups of O'odham were hired to help build the short lines at Ray and near Bisbee-Naco, both in Arizona Territory. Later, O'odham traveled as far as El Paso, Texas, and Las Vegas, Nevada, to work for the railways. Although temporary and distantly located, railroad work still offered better wages to the O'odham than jobs closer to the reservations.

In the early decades of the twentieth century, the O'odham also took construction jobs building dikes and levees on the Colorado River to control the water flow to the Salton Sea. They also worked on a federal dam project near Yuma. During this time, the government played an active part in finding employment for the O'odham, and as part of this effort, the government sent several groups to Rocky Ford, Colorado, to work in the sugar beet fields.

As the O'odham entered the twentieth century, they found themselves in a situation where they were less able to sustain their old way of life based on farming and gathering. Increasingly, they turned elsewhere to make a living. Some turned to raising cattle, but this could not be successful over the long run because the grasslands could not support enough cattle for everyone to make a decent living. Others looked to employment as cowboys, railroad laborers, construction workers, and domestics. There was never enough employment available to make a good living, but with their traditional skills supplemented by the available wages, they were able to survive.

# 8

## *A Home on the Range*

*And I told my mother they were going to send me to another school.*
*So they brought some boys from the reservation and we get together,*
*you know. And my little brother about six years old, he wanted to go*
*and he cried, you know, and so we took him. My little brother slept all*
*the way. I don't know which way he went—which way the train went.*
*I don't remember. We arrived in Santa Fe. We spent five years there. I*
*was fourteen years old. My brother was about eleven.*

JAMES MCCARTY, Interview

*Once there were people coming around picking up kids to go to*
*school but they (the elders) prevented us from going. Nowadays*
*knowing how to speak English is the devil's way. No good. Can bring*
*harm. We don't speak any English.*     TULPO ZUNNIE, Interview

The second decade of the twentieth century was a momentous period
for the O'odham, and they experienced significant changes as they
drew closer to the U.S. government and the people who were their
new neighbors.

The international border created a greater division among the
O'odham because of political events that led to conflict and, eventually, the erection of a fence. Education became more widely available
and was often a matter of students attending day schools rather than
leaving family and home to attend a boarding school. Previously, only
students of families living on the reservation at San Xavier were able
to attend school close to home because the mission provided the
school. For others, life away from home and family had been the only
way to receive an education.

Between 1917 and 1919, World War I drew O'odham men into the
army, and they experienced war on a distant continent. They also
were taken far from their lands for training. This gave young adult
O'odham exposure to cultural differences within the United States,
and those who traveled abroad learned of the differences in the lands
where they fought. Although the changes did not alter the lives of the

people overnight, they were factors that would slowly bring about vast changes in the O'odham traditions. Probably the most important event was the creation of a large reservation that encompassed most of the lands that the O'odham still used.

During the last decade of the nineteenth century and the first two decades of the twentieth century, a period of reform developed within the United States called the Progressive Era. Progressives realized that there were many problems that needed to be solved within the United States, and various groups of people proposed a broad spectrum of reform. They sought reform in government, industries, education, social services, and almost any organization that involved people.

As part of the Progressive movement, a group of eastern liberals with a social conscience began to push for Indian rights. They believed that the United States had been less than honorable in dealing with the native populations as the expansion westward displaced the Indians, and they felt that the government had set up the allotment system to further rob the Indians of their reserved lands. As mentioned in chapter 7, after allotments were made, the government opened for settlement the remainder of the reservations that participated in the allotment process. Anyone who claimed and paid for the land could own and settle it.

Some of the Progressives who were interested in Indians established an organization headquartered in Philadelphia called the Indian Rights Association. This organization was active in advocating the independence of Indian tribes and in trying to see that no government entity diminished the rights they did have. Indians still had traditions (most of which the government was attempting to change), land, and in some cases, treaties that guaranteed compensation for loss of land.

The members of the Indian Rights Association attempted to persuade Congress to treat the Indians fairly. This often involved mustering support from eastern Progressives to counter the congressional delegations from the West, who wanted the reservations reduced or the Indians removed altogether from their states or territories.

With support from the Indian Rights Association, a group of O'odham in 1911 created the first political organization that would represent all O'odham in the United States. The people who formed the group, called the Good Government League, were mostly from the southeast section of what is now the reservation, and many were former students of off-reservation schools. Many also belonged to the

Presbyterian church. For a number of years, this organization was successful in helping the O'odham present their concerns to the Indian Bureau and government officials in a unified and forceful manner. The Good Government League often supported government programs for the O'odham.

However, the O'odham did not always appreciate the policies of the federal government. Many of them did not like being pushed in the direction the government wanted them to go. To counter the influence of the Good Government League, opponents formed an alternative organization with the intent of promoting conservative O'odham values. This organization was the League of Papago Chiefs. Most of its members were Catholics who had spent less time away from the reservation. Its purpose was to oppose many of the changes fostered by the Good Government League and the federal government, which the Indian Bureau implemented through established policies. The League of Papago Chiefs developed considerable power, and in the 1920s, the group had enough clout to have a superintendent removed from the reservation.

In the two decades or so of its existence, the Good Government League exerted some influence and aided in the decision to set aside land for day schools on the main reservation. By executive order in 1911, President Taft designated four little parcels of land for schools and an agency. Three of these sites for the schools and the agency were at Indian Oasis, and the other at San Miguel. The order set aside eighty acres of land at each village.

While Congress considered the matter of a larger reservation for the O'odham, executive orders set aside more O'odham lands. Finally, in 1914 Congress appropriated $50,000 for schools at Chuichu, Cockleburr, Gila Bend, Indian Oasis, San Miguel, and Santa Rosa. By 1916, all were completed except the one at San Miguel, and two others were under construction at Kohatk and Vamori. Some mission schools supported by the Catholic and Presbyterian churches also were available to teach the O'odham children.

In fact, the Catholic church operated the first day school for the O'odham children in the desert area that was to become the main reservation. Father Bonaventure Oblasser, a dedicated Franciscan friar, laid the foundations for a day-school system among the O'odham. In 1912, the first day school began in Little Tucson. An O'odham teacher, Mrs. Margaret J. Norris, provided the instruction. Later the same year, the Catholics opened a school at Topawa. To make these schools successful, the O'odham dug the wells for water, built or donated the building in which classes were to be held, and supplied the teachers. The teachers at St. Anthony's in Topawa were Laura Juan and Minnie Avalos, O'odham women with fourth-grade educations.

As time went on, the Catholics established more schools. They started schools at San Miguel, Chuichu, and Gila Bend within two years. Still later, day schools opened at Cowlic, Cababi, and Anegam. Although the Catholic schools closed when the government opened a school in the same village, the O'odham had begun to perceive education as vital because of these early schools. (Sometimes schools closed when the mines that had attracted workers shut down and left villages deserted, as was the case with San Solano at Cababi in 1918.)

In 1916, the agent at San Xavier Reservation said in his annual report that he was well satisfied with the work done by the mission schools. He also reported that the reservation schools were following the curriculum of the Arizona public schools, with some modifications to fit the O'odham children. He noted that the students who returned from boarding schools in other areas often had to leave the reservation and their lands in order to find employment that would use the skills they had learned. Those schools taught carpentry, woodworking, welding, iron-working, baking, and home economics, skills that seldom could be used profitably on the reservation. This took the better-educated O'odham away from the reservation.

To encourage educated young people to remain on the reservation, the superintendent suggested that most O'odham children be taught on or near their place of residence and that they should learn agricultural techniques that could be used to improve the conditions of their people. However, the problem was not solved, and educated people continued to leave the reservation. Agriculture played a continually decreasing role in the O'odham economy, and there were few opportunities on the reservation for well-educated O'odham other than teaching and tribal administration.

Although agriculture diminished in relative importance among the O'odham, cattle raising increased. Weather in the 1890s caused great damage among the herds of both the O'odham and the Anglo ranchers, and the economic depression of those years reduced demand and lowered prices. Therefore, profits from cattle went down. Many of the Anglos left. Those who remained suffered more trouble in 1904, when another drought severely reduced the herds.

Conflicts with other ranchers had lessened somewhat since the turn of the century, but there was still competition for range and especially for water. As the O'odham cattlemen slowly rebuilt their herds, they impressed the government officials as well as the Indian Rights Association with their ability to handle cattle, and the advocates of the O'odham were able to convince Congress to appropriate money to develop water for the so-called nomadic Papagos who lived west of the San Xavier Reservation.

In 1914, Congress sent $5,000 to develop a water supply for stock and domestic purposes, and then continued to appropriate similar or increased amounts. Appropriations totaled as much as $40,000 in some years. These government funds paid for the drilling of deep wells at Topawa, Indian Oasis, Vamori, San Miguel, Santa Rosa, Anegam, Kohatk, Tat Momelik, Cockleburr, Chuichu, and Gu Komelik. The government built most of the schools near these wells and installed pumping stations to bring water to the surface throughout the year. The water and schools enticed the O'odham to maintain year-round homes, and they began to build permanent structures as houses, usually of adobe. However, they still traveled often for work opportunities or celebrations.

The success of the O'odham cattle raisers did more than bring money for water improvements. The superintendents of the Papago Reservation at San Xavier and the inspectors who traveled to see the non-reservation O'odham cited this success as an indication of how advanced and industrious the O'odham were. As Indian Bureau employees and Indian Rights Association members began pushing for protection of O'odham rights to land, the fact that they had substantial herds of cattle played a major role in determining the size of the reservation proposed for them.

Range studies had determined that each head of cattle needed about 140 acres of the dry desert land to sustain it for a year; therefore, any reservation set aside for the O'odham would have to be large if it were to support cattle ranching as a major industry.

The first formal attempt at providing lands for the O'odham west of San Xavier was through allotments. In 1910, the government sent a special agent to allot 160 acres to each of the O'odham living in that part of Arizona Territory. The O'odham benefited from the amendment to the General Allotment Act, which Congress passed in 1891. This act limited the size of allotments to 80 acres except for grazing lands, which could be double that amount. However, even if all the

O'odham had received the maximum acreage allowed, it would not have been enough for each family to raise more than a few cattle.

The agent sought out the best grazing lands in the desert between San Xavier and Ajo, and he proposed allotting contiguous plots to the O'odham. By 1914, he had surveyed nearly three thousand proposed allotments throughout the valleys of the Papaguería. These blocks of land, which had been assigned to individuals, then became the basis of a series of proposed reservations, but in the end, the government rejected these proposals in favor of a large reservation. The secretary of the interior never approved the allotments anyway, and the process was a failure, like the earlier allotment attempt at Gila Bend. The O'odham would have to wait for a reservation. Fortunately, they did not have to wait long.

A reservation that would sustain the existing herds that some of the O'odham had developed would take a large section of land. On January 14, 1916, President Woodrow Wilson set aside approximately 2.75 million acres of land in southern Arizona as the Papago Reservation. The reservation was the second largest set aside for Indians in the United States. It included nearly half of Pima County and parts of Maricopa and Pinal counties in Arizona. It stretched from the crest of the Baboquivari range almost to Ajo, and from the Mexican border nearly to Casa Grande. Within that block of land, only the land of the Santa Rosa Cattle Company was excluded from the reservation.

Also included within the reservation was an arm of land that reached into the Avra Valley eastward toward Tucson. This section of land became known as the Garcia Strip and was added because relatives of Jose X. Pablo, a member of the committee set up to give advice about creating the reservation, lived there. Pablo wanted his relatives' lands included within the reservation. The whole valley had been part of the O'odham lands, but because of a lack of permanent water sources, the O'odham had no villages there. The farms that the Garcias created were made possible because of an earlier Indian agent who wanted the O'odham in Tucson to move away from the city and its potentially harmful influences. To accommodate the move, the government drilled a deep well on this land to make farming possible, so the Garcias and others settled the area.

Besides Pablo, several other members of the committee recommended lands for the proposed reservation. They were Frank Thackery, the Indian agent at Gila River Reservation; the Reverend F. S. Herndon, Presbyterian missionary; Father Bonaventure Oblasser,

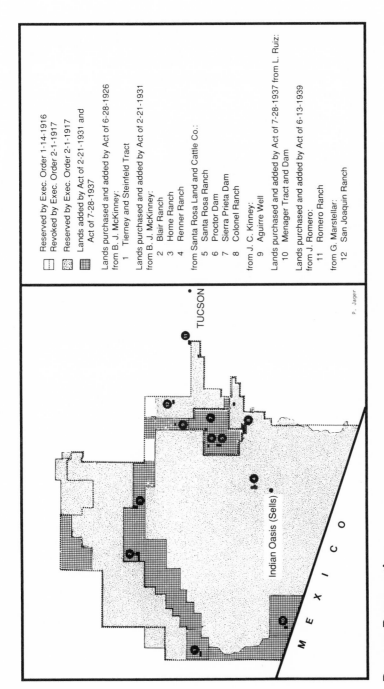

**Papago Reservation**

☐ Reserved by Exec. Order 1-14-1916
⬚ Revoked by Exec. Order 2-1-1917
▨ Reserved by Exec. Order 2-1-1917
▦ Lands added by Act of 2-21-1931 and Act of 7-28-1937

Lands purchased and added by Act of 6-28-1926 from B. J. McKinney:
1  Tierney and Steinfeld Tract

Lands purchased and added by Act of 2-21-1931 from B. J. McKinney:
2  Blair Ranch
3  Home Ranch
4  Renner Ranch

from Santa Rosa Land and Cattle Co.:
5  Santa Rosa Ranch
6  Proctor Dam
7  Sierra Prieta Dam
8  Colonel Ranch

from J. C. Kinney:
9  Aguirre Well

Lands purchased and added by Act of 7-28-1937 from L. Ruiz:
10  Menager Tract and Dam

Lands purchased and added by Act of 6-13-1939 from J. Romero:
11  Romero Ranch

from G. Marstellar:
12  San Joaquin Ranch

P. Jager

TUCSON

Indian Oasis (Sells)

M E X I C O

Jose X. Pablo, stockman, Papago Reservation (Courtesy of the National Archives,
RG 75, Sells, 23245-20-047)

Catholic missionary; Henry J. McQuigg, Indian agent at San Xavier
Reservation; Charles R. Olberg, Bureau of Indian Affairs irrigation
engineer; John R. T. Reeves, representative of the Indian Bureau in
Washington, D.C.; and another influential O'odham member, Hugh
Norris. The work these people did in determining what to include in
the reservation, and then convincing the necessary people to have it
created, is truly impressive.

Creation of the reservation certainly did not return all of their lands
to the O'odham. None of the land in Mexico could be set aside for
their use, and a large portion of the area they used in the United States
was not included. Perhaps a quarter of the O'odham country, as recognized in Kino's time, became the reservation. Areas that the allotting agent recommended earlier, such as most of the Avra and Altar
valleys, the Ajo area, and Quitobaquito, did not remain in the final
draft.

Nevertheless, creation of the reservation caused considerable criticism. Newspapers in Arizona, such as the *Citizen,* objected to the size and the loss of potential tax income from the land. The cattlemen who had run their cattle on the public domain lands that were now to be set aside as the reservation immediately began to complain to their elected governmental officials to have the reservation reduced drastically.

Not every non-Indian was against the founding of the reservation though. The writers of the *Arizona Daily Star* took a moderate stance and noted that removing the land from county responsibility would lessen Pima County's expenses in the areas of Indian affairs, law and order, and health services provided to the O'odham. Also, the federal government would take over the responsibility for building the roads, schools, hospitals, and other services on the reservation. These capital improvements also would bring money to the county because they would otherwise have to be paid for out of county and state taxes.

However, the opposition voices to the reservation were louder and more effective than the moderate ones. Because of the uproar over the size of the reservation, in February 1917, President Wilson reduced the size considerably by another executive order. This action divided the reservation in half, with a strip averaging about seven miles wide cutting an east-west corridor through the center. In all, the executive order returned 475,000 acres in that strip to the public domain. Eventually, the government would restore those lands, but the fact that they were removed shows the displeasure and power of those who did not want the lands in Indian hands.

The raising of livestock, which was a major factor in bringing the reservation into existence, did not come without detrimental effects. Although it allowed a free-ranging way of life for those engaged in it, which suited the traditional O'odham ways well enough, cattle raising also created divisions among the O'odham. The loss of sharing, a major part of O'odham lives since anyone can remember, was mentioned earlier. Also, the environmental damage continued. The desire for profit and surplus, as opposed to traditional O'odham values, increased as cattlemen became more and more successful. Greed, of course, became a potential source of discord within the O'odham community.

Range quality continued to decline from overgrazing, and drought years were particularly hard on the desert ecology. The O'odham would have to learn, as would the Anglos, that the range had limits as to how many animals it would support. Also, the constant drawing of

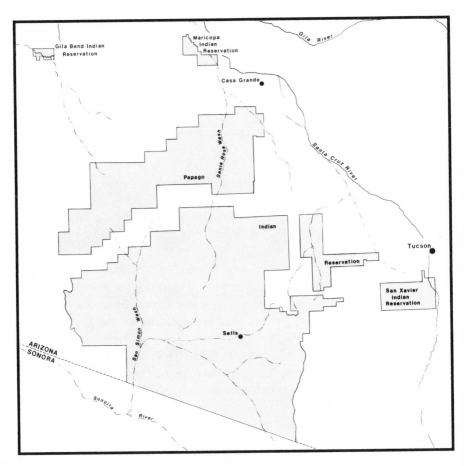

## Tohono O'odham lands, 1919

water from wells could not be done without depleting the underground water supply. Unfortunately, people usually learn such lessons after too much damage has been done.

Because the O'odham were known for their effective desert agriculture and their cattle raising but had little interest in mining, the committee that recommended the lands as a reservation decided to recommend that the O'odham be given surface rights only. This would allow grazing and farming. The O'odham made this concession to increase the chances that the government would approve the reservation. Thus, mineral rights would remain open to prospectors and developers from off the reservation, and by filing mining claims, Anglos would still be able to gain control over some reservation lands. They also could build access roads and make other changes on the land that would be necessary for their mining activities.

The reservation finally had been created, but the problems were just beginning. It would take years before the legal system and Congress would solidify rights to the reservation, eliminate the dividing strip, and give the O'odham rights to minerals found upon their land.

Although the O'odham now had a reservation that somewhat protected their lands, they still were in desperate need of means to support themselves. The standard of living by which they would be judged by others, and to some extent by themselves, was the norm of the non-Indians in the neighboring towns.

When measured by income earned, cattle ranching was a successful enterprise for only a few O'odham families. Others raised enough cattle to supply their families with meat, but they certainly did not profit greatly from cattle sales. Many preferred to raise horses because ownership of horses brought prestige. Farming put some food on the tables of those who still planted, but it could not produce much income for the O'odham. Even though the O'odham often won prizes for their vegetables in county fairs, a few excellent examples of produce did not provide a viable agricultural economy for the entire O'odham population.

Events far away from the lands of the O'odham also brought changes to their lives. The development of the pneumatic tire, which was rubber supported by cotton belts made with long-staple cotton, was such an event.

Manufacturers had to import most long-staple cotton from Egypt, and doing so cost a great deal. About 1910, New England textile mills were importing about $20 million worth of Egyptian cotton a year. However, in 1915, when Europe became engaged in war, imports of Egyptian cotton slowed down significantly.

In the meantime, the cotton industry in Arizona grew rapidly. As early as 1907, experiments at Sacaton had shown that long-staple cotton would grow in southern Arizona. Although the industry was extremely labor intensive, it was only for two seasons of the year. Spring planting demanded extra labor, but the enormous labor demands came during the late fall and early winter, when workers had to pick the mature cotton.

Picking cotton was an attractive kind of work that enticed many O'odham who, like other Indians of southern Arizona, were often either unemployed or underemployed. Also, they were accustomed to migrating seasonally for labor opportunities, and the work in the cotton fields was something in which the whole family could participate.

Cotton picking did have some drawbacks though. Children had to leave the schools they attended on the reservation, and parents discouraged their children from attending schools near the cotton fields because their help in the fields was financially beneficial.

The Indian Bureau and its agents did what they could to arrange favorable terms for the Indian labor. The bureau also attempted to monitor farm conditions to see that living standards were reasonably sanitary. As a precondition for hiring Indian workers, certain restrictions applied to growers, including the prohibition of alcoholic beverages for the Indians. Everywhere the Indian workers went, the temptation of alcohol was difficult to avoid, and unscrupulous dealers offered it to Indians regardless of regulations. Greed, which the non-Indians had introduced, was a major characteristic of the intruding culture and was a factor in relationships whenever the two groups met.

The Indian Bureau officials were convinced that the cotton industry would be the vehicle that would pull the O'odham and Pima Indians out of poverty and raise their standard of living. Unfortunately, it did not raise the living standard very far. The Indian labor benefited the cotton industry and the owners of the cotton fields, but at the expense of the workers. Wages bought barely enough food to survive, and the labor was seasonal, so during long periods of unemployment, workers had to use any savings.

However, the cotton-industry spokesmen had so much power that the Indian Bureau officials often ignored the best interests of the O'odham to assure the cotton owners that they would have workers. In 1916, Frank Thackery, who had been on the reservation committee, wrote that the labor that the O'odham supplied the cotton industry was one of the main reasons why the government established the reservation. He said at least a thousand O'odham pickers would be needed in September of that year, and if the O'odham had a reservation, there would be an administration in place to recruit and organize workers for the cotton producers.

Also in 1916, the superintendent of the reservation wrote to the commissioner of Indian affairs and reported that the New Cornelia

Mines at Ajo were hiring O'odham workers. A railroad had been completed to the mine, and expansion was going to be rapid, with up to three thousand mine workers in the near future. The company hired mostly Mexicans, but the manager told the superintendent that the O'odham were good workers and he would hire them if they were interested.

The Ajo mines could have taken most of the unemployed on the reservation and supplied permanent jobs with the promise of adequate housing, schools, and competitive wages rather than temporary cotton field positions, but the government did not encourage the O'odham to go into mining. Although officials in the Indian Bureau said the environment would be detrimental to the O'odham's health and welfare, occasionally they recommended mining jobs if the company agreed that the O'odham would be free to go to the cotton fields for the planting and harvesting seasons. As World War I spurred the growth of the cotton and mining industries, the number of O'odham in both occupations increased.

The entrance of the United States into World War I also had another effect on the O'odham. The government required the O'odham to register for the draft, inducted many of them into the military forces, and sent some of them abroad. Fifteen O'odham men fought in World War I, and one of them was Joseph McCarthy (later known as James McCarty), who was wounded and captured in Belgium and sent to a prisoner of war camp in Rastatt, Germany.

The political turmoil of the revolutions in Mexico also caused concern. The followers of Vanustiano Carranza and Francisco (Pancho) Villa kept northern Mexico in a state of agitation and warfare during World War I, and the rumors that Mexico would join Germany and attack the United States kept everyone on the border worried.

In June 1915, the superintendent at San Xavier recommended that O'odham men be admitted into the Arizona National Guard, but military officials informed him that the O'odham were not wanted and would not be accepted. In September of the same year, Jose X. Pablo advised that some protection was needed for the O'odham in the desert. They lived near seventy-five miles of the unfenced, unpatrolled international boundary, and their cattle made tempting targets for the Mexican forces on the other side.

For the next four years, the reservation superintendents constantly worried that problems would develop, and they continued to ask the

Indian Bureau and the army for military patrols on the reservation or arms for the O'odham. They never received either. Neither the army nor the Indian Bureau wanted to place guns in the hands of Indians.

For many years previous to the war, the O'odham on both sides of the international border and the Mexicans who lived near the boundary rounded up the cattle every six months. American cattle often crossed into Mexico, where there were more permanent water sources, but once the cattle were together, each owner could find those marked with his brand and separate them from the common herd. Then the calves could be identified, branded, and returned to the range.

In 1916, however, the O'odham attempted to round up the cattle as usual, but a company of Carranza's men would not allow them to cross into Mexico. Reports surfaced that the Mexicans were killing and eating the cattle, and driving the horses farther south so they could not be retrieved by their rightful owners from the United States.

For three years, the O'odham, through their superintendents, attempted to regain possession of their cattle through diplomatic avenues. By the time they were successful, there was not much left of their herds. They must have longed for the days some sixteen or seventeen years before when, faced with a similar problem, they armed themselves and retrieved their cattle by force. This time, however, they were facing well-armed soldiers, and they probably would not have had such success. Throughout these years, the O'odham continued to report that Mexican soldiers and bandits were crossing the border to steal livestock, to buy food supplies, or to smuggle guns and ammunition into Mexico.

The Mexicans used gold dust or alcohol to purchase what they needed. Arizona, which had become a state in 1912, had voted to become a dry state by 1914, and no alcoholic beverages could be sold legally there. People still were allowed to make alcoholic beverages for their own consumption, but many people found it simpler to buy from the Mexicans, who were eager to smuggle liquor across the largely unwatched boundary.

By 1918, even before the ill-fated Eighteenth Amendment to the U.S. Constitution brought Prohibition to the entire country, Arizonans had voted to prohibit even home-brewed liquor. The market was therefore profitable and tempting for Mexicans, and with the border unguarded, smuggling across the reservation became popular.

Try as they might, the superintendents could not get any support from the War Department or the Indian Bureau. When the O'odham

O'odham footrace, 1919. Relay and individual races were major forms of entertainment and social interaction among the O'odham. (Photograph by Edward H. Davis, courtesy of Museum of the American Indian, Heye Foundation)

saw Mexican soldiers or smugglers on the reservation, they had to notify the agency, and then the agent had to inform the commander in charge of the army unit in Nogales. There were no telephones on the reservation, and few automobiles, so it took several days before an army patrol reached the reservation. By then, of course, the Mexicans had done what they came to do and returned to Mexico.

While the government did not take much interest in protecting the O'odham from possible Mexican attacks, it was interested in protecting the O'odham from what was considered wrongdoing. As mentioned earlier, the absence of alcohol was considered a requirement for a company that wanted Indian workers.

The Indian agency also tried to prohibit gambling. The importance of developing large herds of cattle for sale already had discouraged many O'odham from the traditional intervillage gambling on footraces, but the Indian agency was also determined to root out gambling on games. People with European culture had introduced card games, which had gained some popularity, and the O'odham played their traditional games using sticks and their form of dice. The agency had little success controlling the games played in the village.

As the Indian agency became more organized and powerful, it tried to provide more services to the O'odham. One of their greatest needs seems to have been treatment of an eye disease called trachoma. The agency physician in 1911 found that more than 61 percent of the students attending the day school had trachoma, and thirty-five of the forty-nine cases were severe enough to require an operation. The other fourteen cases were suspected or beginning and could be controlled through topical treatment. At that time, the agency physician seldom, if ever, traveled to the non-reservation O'odham, so it is impossible to know how bad the disease was elsewhere. Trachoma continued to be a problem until the O'odham regularly lived in better housing and obtained better eye care.

The O'odham were also affected by the worldwide influenza epidemics of 1918 and 1919. Although there is not much information about influenza on the main reservation, in 1918, at the day school in San Xavier, there were 127 reported cases of Spanish influenza. Eight of those who became ill developed pneumonia, and one pupil and one Pima volunteer employee died.

In 1919, in Tucson, one of the field matrons reported more than 30 deaths among the O'odham living there. Other matrons dealing with the young women who were placed as domestic workers reported some cases of the flu but few deaths. In Ajo, unofficial sources reported more than 300 cases of flu. Some workers in the cotton fields also reportedly fell ill, but apparently most of the victims survived, because there were no reports of deaths in the official correspondence.

As the government stressed its health programs and built hospitals, the O'odham slowly began to accept the government doctors' help. In the early years, that help probably was not much more effective than the traditional O'odham healer, but as medical advances were made, and new, effective drugs were developed to counteract infections, more of the O'odham began to accept and benefit from government medical assistance.

At first, most of the services were located on the San Xavier section of the reservation, but the government eventually extended services to the western area and decided to establish a new agency at Indian Oasis. The government already had drilled wells to supply the school there, but the agency was going to bring in several employees and their families, so it had to drill more wells. The government also had to erect and furnish houses and office buildings.

Finally, on March 1, 1919, the agency officially began to operate in the new location. The O'odham agreed to rename Indian Oasis and call the village Sells, after Cato Sells, the commissioner of Indian affairs at the time the reservation was established. The superintendent wrote to the post office and explained that the agency had been moved and the name of the village had been changed. He requested that mail be delivered at least three times a week rather than once a week, as before, so that the office could run more effectively.

During the second decade of the twentieth century, the O'odham gained some recognition of their rights to exist on a section of their original lands, and the government established a large reservation for them. They then saw the reservation attacked by the same government that created it, and they witnessed a large chunk of it taken back. It would take the next two decades to settle the boundaries of the reservation, but eventually the O'odham would regain the land that executive orders had removed. They were even able to add bits and pieces of land to the original grant. Meanwhile, the O'odham lands became a target for a bizarre takeover attempt that would take several years of court battles to resolve.

In 1914, a Robert M. Martin, through his attorneys, filed suit in Washington, D.C., to clear title to some two million acres of O'odham land. Apparently, a former Union Army colonel named Robert F. Hunter had visited the O'odham in the 1880s as an investigator for the director of the Catholic Bureau of Indian Missions. As well as can be determined through stories that surfaced, Hunter learned that the O'odham were living on public domain lands, and he negotiated with the O'odham leaders the right to secure for them a clear and legal title to all their lands. Hunter had some deeds written and allegedly signed by various chiefs, who later insisted that they knew nothing of them. In payment for his services, the O'odham allegedly were to give Hunter half of the lands he secured for them.

Hunter unsuccessfully tried to gain legal recognition for an O'odham land title, and he finally sold most of his interest in the lands to Martin for $6,000. Martin then pursued his claims in court. However, even before the case was decided, Martin began selling plots of land to raise money to continue the legal proceedings. The case reached the Supreme Court, which remanded the case back to the Washington, D.C., courts, and the case was never legally decided. Finally, in 1930, the Department of the Interior issued a memorandum indicating that although the courts had not ruled, the intent of the courts was that the case had no merit and that the deeds were worthless. However, the legal battles to secure the reservation still lay ahead.

The problems with Mexico persisted to the end of the decade, but after the end of World War I, tensions on the border eased somewhat. Germany was no longer a threat and could not support Mexico, and therefore Mexico was much less a concern.

However, the Yaqui Indians of Sonora had begun smuggling arms and ammunition to aid in their continued struggles against Mexico over their legal and property rights, and Mexican officials alleged that the O'odham were helping them. The agent and other investigators found no proof of that, but finally the Bureau of Indian Affairs decided it was time to fence the border along the reservation line. The bureau would supply the materials, but it expected that the O'odham would supply the labor.

At last the border would be secure for the protection of livestock, but the fence physically separated the O'odham of Mexico from those in the United States. In theory, they continued to have unrestricted access across the border, but as times changed, that access would become less free.

The second decade of the twentieth century drew to an end with the O'odham in a completely different situation than at the beginning of the decade. The next period would see them change more: they would fight to regain the part of the reservation they had lost, they would learn to deal with the legal system of the United States, and they would begin to develop a government of a completely different nature than they had known before.

# 9

## Drought, Unemployment, and Survival

*I used to hear those songs coming from the houses, because we were
so happy in summertime. We had rain. Every morning the sky was
bright and every afternoon the little white cloud stood over the mountains to the east. Everywhere by the washes you saw the centipedes
that are a sign of rain. We call them a blessing, those centipedes. There
were so many that you could shake your head and, pff! one would fall
out of your hair. Now there are no more. That fine weather is gone.*

RUTH M. UNDERHILL, *Papago Woman*

The 1920s were the major formative years for modern O'odham society and government. Many changes in the social and cultural aspects
of the lives of the O'odham had begun earlier, but increased assimilation of non-Indian values and traditions occurred because of education,
economic factors, and close association with the dominant culture.

Change across the broad spectrum of the O'odham Nation varied
according to location and education. The O'odham in San Xavier, of
course, were more exposed to cultural differences than were those
on the Sells reservation. However, those who lived in or around Sells
gradually became more exposed to those differences through the
agency and the federal government's personnel.

The least affected were those who lived in the far western and
northwestern sections of the reservation. Even there, Ajo was a major
influence because the cultural traits of Anglo-American and Mexican
workers in the mines continually influenced O'odham workers.

About the time the O'odham were turning to the use of horse-
drawn wagons, the Anglos were turning to automobiles, which became very popular and brought more non-Indians onto the reservation. The roads of the reservation actually were quite good for the
time. The dry desert environment and supportive soils made smooth
and flat roads except when rain turned them into slippery or rutty
messes.

O'odham women playing toka, a traditional O'odham game (Courtesy of Venito Garcia Library, Sells)

However, because automobiles needed support services such as gas stations and mechanics, they were still not practical for the O'odham, who generally lived far from these facilities. Instead, the O'odham used wagons for transportation. The wagons were useful to haul people as well as goods to markets, to visit relatives, or to go to favorite festivals such as the feast of Saint Francis held on October 4 in Magdalena, Sonora, Mexico.

Housing changed slowly and first began to imitate that of the Mexicans or Hispanics. Rectangular adobe houses with small windows were the choice of most O'odham as they set up permanent residence in a village, and they abandoned the brush shelters and mud shelters of earlier periods. The Anglo-American's frame houses did not appeal to the O'odham until the advent of effective air-conditioning systems because such houses were either too hot or too cold. Adobe houses moderated the temperature much better and therefore were more comfortable during either the hot or cold seasons.

In the style of clothing, the O'odham again usually followed the fashion of the Mexicans. The men wore trousers, shirts, and large hats, and many of them cut their hair. Women wore long skirts with blouses, and they grew long hair that they continued to wash with the soap weed from the Baboquivari Mountains. (For conditioning, the O'odham women massaged cows' brains into their hair.)

Most of the agent and field matron reports indicate that these officials generally considered the O'odham clean and tidy. Peter Blaine remembers that when his family lived on the outskirts of Tucson, his mother was washing nearly all the time and would not allow him or his stepfather to wear a shirt more than once without cleaning it.

After World War I ended, the country's economy fell into a recession. For many areas and in much of the economy, the recession was short, and prosperity returned with a flourish. However, as manufacturing enjoyed banner success through much of the Roaring Twenties, as this period has been called, not all segments of society participated in the good times. To survive, the O'odham had to look to various sources of income.

The O'odham often traveled to towns like Bisbee, Arizona, to sell their handmade baskets and *ollas,* or pots. They also established roadside markets and sold their goods to passersby. The O'odham who had small herds of cattle made jerky by drying thin strips of meat in the sun, which they sold to the O'odham, Yaquis, and Mexicans on

Brush shelters with tarp modifications (Courtesy of Venito Garcia Library, Sells)

the southwestern fringe of Tucson. All of these products were labor-intensive and did not bring much profit, but still, they helped keep some families going.

The agriculture business basked in high prices during the war and shortly after, but when the warring countries ceased to fight, people were able to return to the business of growing food. When their crops were ready for harvest, the boom for the farmers of the United States was over. Of course, that meant a downturn in prices not only for farm products but also cattle. The O'odham were hit as hard as any other food producers in the United States, and the cattle producers on the reservation lost the profits they had expected.

Although the agricultural economy was bad for most farmers, the O'odham farmers and cattle raisers suffered even more because they were also hit by exceedingly bad weather. In 1921, a severe drought devastated the herds on the reservation because the pumps that the government had drilled the previous decade did not supply enough water. One reason was that the size of the O'odham herds had grown much larger than before the war, but also the pump motors were unre-

O'odham women carrying ollas to market (Courtesy of Venito Garcia Library, Sells)

Cruel effects of a drought on the O'odham's cattle (Courtesy of Venito
Garcia Library, Sells)

liable and constantly in need of repair. Many of the wells went dry
even if the pumps worked.

Cattlemen attempted to save some of the animals by taking them to
the mountains, but even there the traditional water sources failed to
provide enough for the cattle. Some of the animals were sold, but they
were in such bad condition that they brought very little money on the
depressed market.

To improve the cattle's chances of survival, the O'odham began
to round up the many scrub horses that populated the range, and
throughout the 1920s, superintendents' reports indicate they disposed
of large numbers of them. The Mexican government bought many of
the horses, but that market disappeared as the Mexicans either lacked
money, turned to automobiles, or decided that they had enough.
Thereafter, the O'odham sold the horses for pet food or glue.

The cattle herds suffered such devastating losses that in 1923, the
superintendent wrote to the Indian Office that the O'odham were
gathering the sun-bleached bones to sell. They hauled the bones by
wagon to Tucson and sold them for $7 a ton. The bones then were
ground and turned into fertilizer. This grisly work was one way that

**121**

cattle owners recouped some money from what were once healthy herds of cattle. To help rebuild the herds, the superintendent requested $5,000 from the Indian Bureau for the O'odham to purchase 125 bulls.

The weather did not cooperate for much of the 1920s, including a severely dry winter in 1923. Because of the lack of rain, many of the O'odham left the reservation to find work. However, the O'odham were fond of planting their fields, and usually no other work would keep them away from their homes during planting season. If conditions were favorable, they would leave their jobs in the cotton fields or mines to return home for planting, and then they would go back to the jobs off the reservation. If the rains did not come, however, they knew there was no point in planting seeds. The ground could not even be prepared without moisture.

The drought continued the following year, and the summer of 1924 was reported to have had the hottest temperatures for many years. The heat destroyed what crops the O'odham planted and threatened the cattle, even though the charcos reportedly had enough water to last until November. This year turned out better than 1921, however, because rains that fell earlier than usual had filled the charcos and improved the water supply.

The rest of the 1920s did not get much attention in the reports of the agents. Apparently the weather was closer to normal. Correspondence between the superintendent and the Indian Bureau indicates that 1929 was a good year for weather and had created favorable range conditions. In one letter, the superintendent said that the good range conditions were a reason to start to rebuild the herds.

Cotton continued to be important, and the Southwestern cotton farmers were able to retain much of the market they had taken from Egypt and India during the war, but the potential overseas competition kept prices down. The Indians, particularly the O'odham and the Pimas, were valued assets of the cotton growers as seasonal workers. Many O'odham moved to the cotton growing areas and remained there the entire year, but wages for cotton workers did not increase much, and most O'odham workers earned barely enough to live.

One large community of O'odham lived near Florence, Arizona. Reports noted that as many as forty children were there and not enrolled in school. The leader of the community, Chief Konerone, was not sympathetic to the pleas of the Indian Office to enroll the children because he had sent his children to boarding school on the Pima Reservation, and two of them died from illnesses contracted there. Although the Indian Office suggested that the chief be tried in an Indian court for obstructing efforts to place children in schools, there are no reports that indicate any action was taken. Still, the suggestion of such action indicates the attitude of the Bureau of Indian Affairs toward the Indians during this period: they were expected to follow whatever rules the agency set for them.

In 1923, when there was no rain after the workers finished in the cotton fields, the O'odham had no prospects for planting successful crops, and they did not want to return to the reservation because there was nothing there for them. However, most of them could not find other employment around the cotton fields, and the superintendent wrote to the commissioner of Indian affairs to ask for aid. The commissioner answered that they should try to find something in the cotton fields and that there was no chance for supplemental relief from Congress. He further blamed the O'odham for not organizing properly to maximize their earning potential. The O'odham, as always, had to find their own way, and they survived through traditional food-gathering, community sharing, and whatever occasional work they could find.

In subsequent years, cotton growers continued to need the Indians' assistance, and the Bureau of Indian Affairs continued recruiting Indian labor for the industry. The bureau recruited Navajos and Apaches along with Pimas and O'odham, but the growers considered the latter two groups the most reliable. In 1922, about 1,100 O'odham found work in cotton fields, and bureau reports indicate that it expected as many the following year.

The superintendent of the Papago Reservation received payment for recruiting workers for one of the cotton growing associations, and in a letter accompanying the payment, the writer complained that other associations were paying chiefs of villages on the reservation to recruit for their growers. The association did not appreciate the competition from other growers for the O'odham workers because it would inevitably raise the cost of labor for the cotton growers.

The San Xavier Reservation constantly had water problems, and in the 1920s much of the farming activity ceased. As mentioned earlier, floods had lowered the channel of the Santa Cruz River so much that irrigation from that source was difficult or impossible. Moreover,

O'odham workers weighing a bag of cotton, 1930s (Courtesy of Venito Garcia Library, Sells)

settlement upriver already had taken most of the water before it reached the reservation. Thus the rich fields that had supported the O'odham, or Sobaipuris, since long before the time of Kino were mostly left idle.

The last years of the 1920s brought experimentation in cotton growing onto the San Xavier Reservation. Frank Rios successfully grew a crop of several acres of cotton and earned a profit in 1929 and 1930. Two other O'odham farmers attempted to grow cotton in those years, but the lack of water hindered their efforts, and neither produced enough to make any money. The amount Rios earned was not enough to induce him or others to continue cotton growing or to try to develop it on a large scale.

Although mining continued to be an important industry, it did not create the demand for labor that it had during the war. Development of the automobile industry in the postwar period did keep mining going to some extent, but the work available was not permanent or reliable. In 1923, the Phelps Dodge Corporation employed about fifty O'odham at the New Cornelia mines in Ajo. They were able to earn $2.40 a day doing basic pick-and-shovel work as miners.

Because of the problems with farming and cattle raising, many of the O'odham cut wood on the reservation to sell in Tucson. They harvested the mesquite trees, loaded the logs and branches onto their wagons, and then drove the long dusty road to Tucson, which was more than sixty miles away from much of the reservation. It usually took a man and team six days to cut a wagon load of wood and transport it to Tucson, and for all that effort, he could earn $6. The wage rate of $1 a day was less than half that of the men working in the mines, but it was the only profitable employment available for many O'odham families.

Domestic service was still a major source of employment for the women who lived in or near Tucson. Of all the types of work available, domestic help may have been the most stable. Some who started as domestic helpers in the 1920s and 1930s continued working into the 1960s and 1970s.

In 1921, a hospital was completed at Sells. It had a forty-four bed capacity, not including the sleeping porch that was added later. It also had central heating and wiring for electricity. With the hospital came improved health care for those of the O'odham who accepted the doctors and care furnished by the Indian Bureau. Some O'odham were willing to accept both traditional cures and modern medicine.

Contagious diseases were still a concern for the O'odham. In January 1923, five persons contracted smallpox in the southern area of the reservation, and three of them died. Officials did not send new pupils to schools in that region while the disease was still present. Most of the children of the reservation already had received vaccinations against smallpox, and no general epidemic developed.

Tuberculosis and the eye disease trachoma were constant problems among the Indians. Trachoma, although not as prevalent among the O'odham as it was among the Navajos, still afflicted many of them. Medicines and operations had been developed that were somewhat effective in controlling the disease, but it still took its toll on the eyesight of Indian peoples until after World War II.

Education continued to be a problem, both for the agency officials and for the O'odham. The Bureau of Indian Affairs wanted to have all the Indians educated in schools that taught a modified public school curriculum. English was the language students were to use in schools, and one of the main purposes of elementary education was to force Indians to learn and to speak English. In some boarding schools, speaking an Indian language was grounds for punishment; educators thought

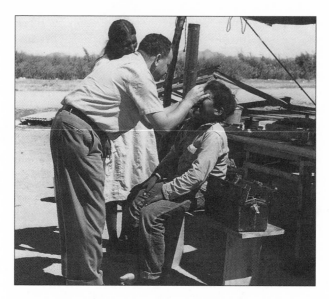

Treating trachoma, a serious eye disease (Courtesy of
Venito Garcia Library, Sells)

the only way for native peoples to progress was to learn English, which
had become the dominant language north of Mexico.

O'odham parents often resisted pressure to send their children to
boarding schools off the reservation, but they still sent many children,
especially for the upper grades. Often the day schools taught only the
first three grades.

Phoenix was the most favored boarding school, although the O'odham sent children to Yuma, Fort Mohave, Haskel Institute, Sherman
Institute, Santa Fe Indian School, and others, all of which actively recruited pupils. The Tucson Indian School, run by the Presbyterian
church, attracted many O'odham children because it was much closer
than the government schools.

The Yuma Indian School was the least favored, and parents often
refused to allow children to go there. Many of the children who
attended Yuma ran away or became ill, and the school gained a
reputation for not having adequate food, clothing, or healthy living
conditions.

The O'odham also had the problem of what to do with the young
adults who returned from distant schools with skills that were not
very useful on the reservation. Many of them had to leave the reserva-

tion to use those skills. In 1923, the Bureau of Indian Affairs asked superintendents to account for the Indian school graduates who had returned to their reservations, and Superintendent McCormick of the Sells agency reported that several of the O'odham graduates were in California, where they had established their own businesses in order to use the school training they had received. Among them were a plasterer and a painter who were doing quite well. In Tucson, there were a couple of graduates employed in tailor shops, and another two working in a lumberyard. One graduate worked at the University of Arizona as a specialist in budding and grafting trees.

If the graduate were male and his family had a fairly large herd of cattle, his education could be useful in dealing with buyers. Education also could have helped people understand how to improve the animals through proper breeding and care. Apparently, the potential existed on the reservation to earn considerable money through cattle ranching if it were done correctly.

One former student returned and assumed control of the family cattle herd, and he did well, reportedly investing $20,000 in three deep wells to supply the animals with water. Unfortunately, the reports to the Indian Bureau that used his case to show the effectiveness of Indian education did not give his name.

Girls who returned from the Indian schools often found employment as domestics in Tucson. Some became teachers' assistants or found work in the hospitals, where they did work similar to that of the domestics.

However, not all of those who received boarding school educations were successful. The superintendent also noted that one graduate was serving a jail sentence in Tucson for burglary.

Education, therefore, was both a benefit and a detriment to the O'odham nation. Some who were educated remained on the reservation and became very influential as tribal government developed. They also became relatively wealthy. Others left the reservation and established themselves in places far removed, and eventually the tribe lost contact with, and the benefit of, some of its most promising young people.

Education was just one of many methods used to pressure the Indians to conform to Anglo cultural norms. During the first three decades of the twentieth century, the Bureau of Indian Affairs made constant attempts to regulate the lives of the native people. Native religions and recreations were not to be practiced, Indians were not to marry in traditional ways, and as mentioned above, language was to be changed—all to make the Indians look just like their new neighbors.

In 1924, the superintendent prohibited the O'odham from dancing later than 11:00 P.M. when school was in session, and he insisted that the custom of dancing through the night was not good for the schoolchildren who, after staying up with their parents, could not perform well in the classroom. He also attributed a number of illnesses and even the deaths of a child or two to the late-night dancing.

Most of these dances were not objectionable as pagan rituals, which the Indian Bureau officials found in other tribes. Usually, they were adapted dances from the Mexicans and even the Anglos, accompanied by a chicken-scratch band of fiddles and drums.

The rain-making ceremony with the drinking of *tiswin,* or cactus wine, was another problem. During the 1920s, the agency constantly tried to prohibit this activity on the reservation. Before the ceremony began, the Indian police on the reservation were to seek out and destroy the wine that the O'odham made from the fruit of the saguaro cactus. Sometimes the police reported that they were successful in stopping the activity. Those who continued the custom, which the traditional O'odham considered necessary to produce the late summer rains, had to do it in secret. No longer could the whole district be invited to these festivities. However, after John Collier became commissioner of Indian affairs in 1933, the bureau stopped trying to destroy Indian religions and ceremonies.

The Indian Bureau believed that eventually, if the Indians changed sufficiently, they would be granted citizenship in this land—the land where they and their ancestors had been born. This push for citizenship was one of the reasons for the General Allotment Act; if the Indians all received land and were successful in developing and using that land, they could then pay taxes like other citizens. They could vote and enjoy whatever privileges citizens enjoyed. They could also sell their land or buy other land if they wanted and could afford it. (Of course, the main reason for the allotment act was to open lands for Anglo settlements, but that is not how the government promoted it.)

Some Indians did become citizens by having their allotments. Then, after World War I, the government noted that some 15,000 Indians had volunteered or had been drafted to serve in the U.S. Army. Fifteen of these were O'odham. Some people felt that if these men were willing to sacrifice their time and perhaps their lives, they should be citizens of the country for which they had fought, and in 1919, Congress

Singing down the rain: the *vi:gida* ceremony (Courtesy of Venito Garcia
Library, Sells)

passed a law extending citizenship to those Indians who had served in
the Allied forces.

In September 1924, President Calvin Coolidge awarded the Papago
tribe a certificate of honor for the tribal contribution to the war effort.
There was an award ceremony in Sells, and the tribe invited the president of the University of Arizona to present the certificate. Of the
fifteen men who had participated in the war, five had died, including
one who had been killed in the war. Five of the others missed the
ceremony because they were off the reservation for employment and
various other reasons, but the remaining five were present. Richard
Hendricks, president of the Good Government League, accepted the
certificate on behalf of the tribe.

Shortly before this award ceremony, Congress had passed an act
giving rights of citizenship to all the Indians who were not yet citizens.
The commissioner immediately wrote to Representative Carl Hayden
of Arizona saying that even with the new law, it was unlikely that

polling places could be erected on Indian reservations, although it would be possible to place them just outside the boundaries. However, polling places near the O'odham lands would have been an empty gesture; the states had much control over the voting privileges and other rights of citizenship, and Arizona and New Mexico did not allow Indians the right to vote until 1948.

In 1924, a group of O'odham men organized the Papago Good Government League, and on November 15, they accepted and ratified its constitution and by-laws. Richard Hendricks was elected president, and Roswell Manuel was appointed vice president. This organization extended the Good Government League, which before had included only the Sells Reservation, to San Xavier and Gila Bend.

A year later, the newly established Council of Tribal Chiefs voiced opposition to the Good Government League because it favored moving in the direction of the federal government's programs. The Council of Tribal Chiefs, on the other hand, was oriented toward maintaining traditional values and customs.

Although members of the various communities on the reservation had the right to choose their leaders, the selection had to be cleared through the superintendent. On September 16, 1927, the superintendent certified and approved the selection of Rocco Esalio as assistant headman, or chief, of the village of Cobabi. This appointment was for as long as he lived or until he resigned, although the members of the village could vote to remove him. This process of election and appointment superseded the traditional practice of communal councils and leadership by reputation.

In the 1920s, the O'odham began their struggle to regain the land taken away by executive order after creation of the initial large reservation. This would prove to be a long process, but it would eventually lead to success. In 1926, the government began buying out Anglos who had claims on the land in the corridor splitting the reservation. The government also purchased most of the alienated original territory of the reservation. This land was returned during the following decade, when many changes for the O'odham and all other Indians were to occur.

On Black Thursday, October 24, 1929, the stock market in New York City experienced a major crash. The following Tuesday, October 29, the market fell even more. Stock values fell drastically and sent the U.S. economy into a tailspin. It would take more than a decade for the country to pull out of its economic depression. The twenties, which had not been a good decade to begin with, ended on an even lower note.

For the O'odham, who had been affected by the agricultural depression that lasted most of the 1920s, the Great Depression was merely an extension of their dismal economic situation. The O'odham were no longer separate from the people of the United States, or even of the world, and always hereafter, the economic condition of the nation would affect the economic well-being of the O'odham and their reservation, too.

# 10

# A Decade of Change

*. . . we go to the saguaro over here and get the saguaro, fix jam, syrup, and the seed—the seeds from the saguaro for our chicken and, also once in a while, we'll grind it and then boil it with the water and put that, the wheat flour, in it like a soup, and it's real good. Eat it. Eat it with bread that they make in those ovens—outside ovens.*

LENA RAMON, Interview

During the United States' devastating depression in the 1930s, the O'odham shared in that economic hardship, but they also experienced some very important developments. They regained control of the land that the government had separated from their main reservation, and they also added some new parcels. Health services improved, and opportunities to attend school on the reservation increased. The cash economy became more prevalent on the reservation as government relief programs brought work there. Perhaps the most important development, however, was the organization of an elected tribal government.

After the stock market crash in 1929, the economy of the United States began a long downward slide into the Great Depression. People throughout the country had difficulty finding work. Many factories closed because people could not afford manufactured goods, which caused more people to lose jobs. The scarcity of jobs forced many people into part-time work, or work for lower wages, and this created competition for positions off the reservation. Cotton picking and the occasional labor in Tucson became difficult to find because so many others who had been laid off from higher paying permanent jobs were willing to take those positions.

During the first three years of the Depression, little was done directly to assist the unemployed. The government did try to stimulate the economy through programs that helped businesses, and perhaps the rich, under the assumption that eventually the benefits would filter down to the needy. That type of aid proved ineffective.

In 1930, Democratic senators had proposed a $15 million food loan for Indians throughout the United States, but when President Hoover threatened to veto the measure, the senators decided not to press the issue. Congress did not pass the bill. The Indian Bureau began a relief program in the autumn of 1931 and requested funds from Congress, but with such a limited program, the O'odham did not receive much help. Earlier, in 1929, the U.S. comptroller general had ruled that landless tribes, which included those tribes whose reservation lands had not been allotted, were ineligible for federal aid. For this reason, the Indian Bureau was slow to initiate programs for Indian relief. Most O'odham had never been allotted, so by this ruling they would have been ineligible for government aid anyway.

It was not until late 1932, when Franklin D. Roosevelt was elected president, that innovative programs began to bring aid and employment to the people who most needed it. Then it took several years of experimentation by trial and error to find programs that worked effectively.

Although the O'odham had been drawn into the wage-earning system, many of them maintained ties to their villages and continued to cultivate their own fields. With good weather, they could grow enough food and gather enough wild food to survive. However, the weather during the early 1930s did not cooperate and was marked by droughts.

By December 1931, the people in the Indian village on the outskirts of Tucson were suffering because of the lack of work, so the superintendent sent a letter to the leaders of the business community and asked them to donate goods or money. He told them that these donations were to be used to help relieve the O'odham who were living near Tucson and to help make their Christmas better. It is not known if there was any response.

Most of the O'odham who had been employed off the reservation returned to their homes when the economic depression became severe. In late spring of 1933, the Emergency Conservation Work program began. This was the first extensive aid program on the reservation, and it enabled government agencies to hire workers for projects on the reservation that improved the range for cattle, and developed water resources for villages and for stock raising. In November 1933, the council representing the Papago tribe had to ask if pipe could be obtained from the Public Works Administration, another relief program, to transport water from sources developed by Emergency Conservation Work projects to where it could be used most effectively.

Food preparation at a cornstalk wind shelter (Courtesy of
Venito Garcia Library, Sells)

The Emergency Conservation Work program employed O'odham
workers throughout the remainder of the decade. Proposals for range
development and erosion control requested more than half a million
dollars in May 1934, and in 1935, the program employed 260 O'odham workers and paid $168,761 in wages.

Also, Congress had passed the Federal Emergency Relief Act in
1933 to help states give relief to citizens, with the federal government
sharing the costs. The program was introduced on the reservation in
1935, but the O'odham who still adhered strongly to traditional ways
had difficulty accepting the work offered by some government officials. For example, a teacher explained the Emergency Relief Act to a
chief in the northwestern section of the reservation, and he answered
that although the people needed work, they would rather starve than
sign their names to the required papers or even answer the questions
the government officials asked.

However, officials went throughout the reservation seeking those
people who were most in need, and they eventually convinced most of
the O'odham who were eligible to sign up for the aid. People even

signed up for the relief projects in Kerwo, in the southwestern part of the reservation, which had the least contact with the culture of the United States.

The Emergency Relief Act became effective on the reservation in January 1935, and by the end of March, the official in charge indicated that O'odham workers had made 20,000 adobe bricks, repaired miles of roads, produced more than 200 comforters and 20 mattresses, and cleaned the agency grounds. The O'odham earned wages for this work, and the items they made were often distributed to other O'odham who needed help. Sometimes the workers received items they produced in place of wages.

In July, the superintendent reported that Emergency Relief Act projects had employed 103 women, and that these women had received $4,460 in wages. They had made 500 comforters, but 409 of them had been issued to the workers as compensation for work performed. The women workers also had produced nearly 900 pieces of clothing to issue to children during the school year.

An agent at Sells reported in August 1935 that the Emergency Relief Act employed 200 men and women between April 1 and July 25 on the Papago Reservation. The average pay was $30 a month. Unfortunately, there was no further work for the program that year. However, the superintendent expected the Emergency Conservation Work program to employ 500 O'odham workers, and the mine at Ajo to reopen within two months with jobs for perhaps 150 men. Road work and cotton picking would supply work for some more of the O'odham. Still, regardless of the work offered though relief programs, there were more than 400 reservation families in which no one was employed.

Congress had also created the Civilian Conservation Corps in 1933, and eventually more than 2.5 million young men participated in this program. The Indian Division, the CCC-ID, was active on the Papago Reservation and gave employment to many O'odham men. Participants worked on range improvements—building more roads, building or improving charcos, and drilling wells.

One interesting project was the building of a fire lookout on top of Baboquivari Peak. CCC-ID workers constructed the Baboquivari lookout complete with a long trail and then ladders to negotiate the difficult last climb to the top. They also added a telephone line to the lookout. However, the Forest Service never used this facility as a fire lookout. After they built it, officials realized there were no forests in the area at great risk of being burned. Grassland fires, should there be any, could be seen readily enough from the valley floor.

One program the reservation did not qualify for was assistance through the Agricultural Adjustment Act. Because of regulations governing the carrying capacity of range, the O'odham had far too many cattle for the size and condition of their range.

In 1938, the average O'odham family earned an estimated $650, which indicates that the O'odham were poorer than most Indian tribes. Non-government employment was responsible for 41 percent of the total income of tribal members, government wage work supplied 20 percent, and the sale of livestock another 18 percent. Farming for family use was valued at about 12 percent of the income. The remaining portion of the estimated income came from the sale of baskets and other handicrafts, the gathering of wild foods, the sale of wood, and other miscellaneous activities.

The government relief programs did more than supply work and wages for the O'odham. The work was an educational experience for

Santa Rosa charco, an example of the improvement projects of the 1920s and 1930s. Charcos are manmade water-retention basins. (Courtesy of Venito Garcia Library, Sells)

Civilian Conservation Corps camp at the base of Baboquivari Peak. Workers developed a trail to the top of the mountain and built a lookout there in the 1930s. (Courtesy of Venito Garcia Library, Sells)

those who were involved. The training received through these projects and participation in wartime activities probably taught the O'odham more skills for dealing with the modern culture than all the educational programs prior to that time.

The camp supervisor for the CCC-ID program at Sells in June 1938 reported that the only training for the reservation projects was done on the job: those who had the most promise received training to do whatever tasks had to be done. This method proved to be quite successful. For example, the supervisor reported that one nine-man crew was employed to install a windmill near San Miguel. All of the crew were O'odham, including the foreman, and they finished the job in good time and did it well. The supervisor felt that many of the workers could easily qualify for jobs off the reservation should employment opportunities become available.

One result of the availability of work in government relief projects was the redistribution of the reservation's population. By 1940, the population of Sells was three times what it had been in 1932. Of course, the tribal government was there, which meant more job

The potter's craft. An O'odham woman shapes a bowl.
(Courtesy of Venito Garcia Library, Sells)

opportunities, and the federal government also hired and stationed people there.

Some tribal leaders pushed to build a tribal community center at Sells. They financed the building with Indian Rehabilitation Trust Funds and Papago Contributed Funds, and constructed it with the co-operation of the CCC-ID. On November 20, 1940, Commissioner John Collier dedicated the building as the Papago Community House, and for many years it served as the activity center of the O'odham people. The tribal community center, the roads, and the water developments are lasting memorials of the Great Depression and the government activities that attempted to relieve the suffering brought by the collapse of the country's economy.

Cattle raising and farming continued to be a major part of the

O'odham's activities during this time, and much of the work that the relief agencies did directly improved the range for cattle and secured water for farming. Agriculture was always risky in the desert, regardless of how extensive the improvements were, but project evaluators noted that the O'odham were skilled desert farmers who could eke out crops where one would least expect success. They also noted that the O'odham were especially fond of planting their fields and would leave any job in order to plant. Only a severe lack of rain could keep them from their traditional planting.

In 1935, one of the relief organization supervisors wrote that the O'odham had not had a good crop year in the last four or five years. Even in normal times, the O'odham could expect only one good crop in three years. To make matters worse, when the crops did not do well, it was usually due to lack of water, which meant the wild foods did not grow well either. Thus, when the crops failed, alternative food sources often were meager, too.

Cattle raisers suffered as much or more through dry periods as those who depended on farming, and many cattle died during the drought prior to 1935. In 1934, the Indian Office granted special permission to use Emergency Conservation Work funds to pump water for livestock. The project watered more than ten thousand head of cattle for seventy days. Seventeen pumping plants worked constantly for more than sixty days and helped save many of the cattle. However, the second half of the decade did not bring much improvement in the weather. The desert experienced another dry winter in 1938, and the cattle were again in poor condition.

During the 1930s, livestock owners tried to improve their range and herds. They not only worked through the relief projects to improve range conditions, but they also continued to round up surplus horses. They gathered and sold nearly a thousand horses in 1936 alone.

Cattle raisers also used reimbursable funds, money for which the tribe applied from the federal government, to purchase purebred bulls. The cattlemen expected the bulls to improve the cattle on the reservation and make them more valuable. The tribe issued the reimbursable funds as low-interest loans to individuals who were expected to repay the money according to a schedule, or when they could. When the borrowers repaid the debt, the tribe could lend the money again.

However, one of the main problems in the desert is the large amount of land necessary to sustain cattle. As noted previously, the range was overstocked and had been for years. Much environmental damage had occurred, and more was to be expected if changes were not made.

According to the reservation superintendent's 1936 annual report, a project to determine the actual stock-carrying capacity of the reservation ranges had been initiated, and it was found that the O'odham had far too many animals grazing on their land. Unfortunately, the results of this project did not change the situation, and the ranges remained overstocked several years later. However, overstocking meant that in the future, it would be impossible to maintain the level of income that the O'odham had been receiving from livestock. The range was losing some of its ability to sustain cattle, and it also was unable to rejuvenate because of the large herds. Cattle could not get fat there.

In the year before August 1939, O'odham cattlemen sold more than 12,000 head of cattle. Although there was still no accurate count, the herd size must have been more than 25,000 head to produce that number of cattle to sell. The recommended carrying capacity of the range was about half that number.

During the 1930s, the O'odham regained much of the land that President Wilson had set aside in 1916 for their reservation. In 1926, the government began to repurchase some of the lands lost in 1917 after President Wilson, in response to strong opposition to the size of the reservation, issued executive orders reducing its size.

In 1930, after the Supreme Court had twice refused to deal definitively with the Hunter-Martin claims, the Department of the Interior issued a memorandum that Martin's claims were without merit and that the United States had title to the land. That cleared the title and ensured that there would be no more claims to the reservation lands that the government had set aside for the O'odham.

The economic depression combined with the droughts of the 1920s and 1930s also severely affected the owners of the lands dividing the reservation, and the situation was desperate for a number of ranchers. Bad weather conditions had resulted in a reduction in the size of the herds, and a weakening of the surviving cattle.

However, the ranchers' hardship benefited the O'odham because they were able to buy back some of those lands dividing the reservation. On February 21, 1931, in response to pressure from the O'odham (particularly the League of Papago Chiefs), the Indian Bureau, and Arizona's congressional delegation, Congress approved an act that enabled the government to buy a number of ranches.

Because of the poor conditions, the ranchers were happy to sell, and the government made a number of purchases. Government agents purchased the Ventana ranch, along with the Blair and Renner ranches, from Ben J. McKinney, who already had sold the Tierney and Steinfeld tract to the government. J. F. Brown sold his lease to the Eldridge ranch. The Santa Rosa Land and Cattle Company gave up the Santa Rosa ranch, which had not been part of the original reservation, and the Colonel ranch. The Santa Rosa company also sold the Proctor and Sierra Prieta dams. Another purchase was the Aguirre well, acquired from J. C. Kinney. With these and other purchases, which reattached or added about 360,000 acres, the reservation regained its unity.

The purchases were complete by 1933, and the northern strip was no longer separated from the southern part of the reservation. As a result, the administration of the northern section returned to the Sells agency from the Pima agency in Sacaton, which had administered that area since the reservation had been divided.

Not all of the land was easily acquired. The Birdie Miller family claimed to have homesteaded land around Kua Katch village in 1935, so when agency employees fenced that land as part of the reservation, the Miller family sued to retain control. However, the O'odham defended their rights to the land, and won in 1938 when the case was tried in court.

The government also bought the Menager Dam tract after Congress approved the purchase and allocated funds in 1937. The Menagers were a family with longstanding ties to the O'odham, and they had operated a trading post at Indian Oasis for many years. In 1908, Joseph Menager had built a dam on the land called Menager's tract, which included the old village of Ak-Chin, the village of Sweetwater, and the village of Camote. O'odham still used these areas for farms and livestock.

Yet even though the O'odham had managed to regain lands that had originally been set aside for them, and even managed to add some small tracts, there were still O'odham who lived off the reservation on lands that were not reserved. Several families still inhabited the area to the west of the reservation, which had been part of the lands of the Hia C'eḍ O'odham.

Some of those lands were lost when President Roosevelt created Organ Pipe Cactus National Monument by a presidential proclamation on April 13, 1937. This act eventually removed 520 square miles of land directly west and bordering the reservation from possible use by the O'odham. For a period after the creation of the national monument, O'odham families retained the right to graze cattle there, but after a few years, the National Park Service withdrew that right.

Also included within the monument was the area of Quitobaquito, which was the location of small springs just inside the U.S. border, from which a stream flowed into Mexico. Quitobaquito was one of the very few places where the Hia C'eḍ O'odham found a reliable water source for growing crops, and there was also a Hia C'eḍ O'odham cemetery there. A couple of families managed to maintain residence at Quitobaquito for a short period of time, and Joseph Orosco and his family stayed until 1955, when the Park Service evicted them and paid them for the loss of their lands.

However, the government was not yet finished locking up lands that the O'odham had traditionally used. In 1939, the United States created the Cabeza Prieta Game Range to protect the desert bighorn sheep, and this effectively removed most of the remaining land in the United States that the Hia C'eḍ O'odham had used. One or two families remained just inside the eastern border of the area, but they found themselves to be illegal squatters on lands their ancestors had occupied for centuries. Mr. Tulpo Zunnie stayed there into the 1990s, but it is unlikely that the government will allow any others to reside on the preserve.

The government finalized the boundaries of the reservation when Congress authorized funds to buy the San Joaquin and Romero ranches in the eastern section. This transaction occurred in 1940 and added 320 acres to the reservation. The Papago Reservation, as it was initially called, was the last reservation that the United States created. Although protests after President Wilson first designated the reservation had caused the government to split it up, at last the government restored those lost areas and solidified the reservation's boundaries.

Still, even though the government had restored the reservation, and enlarged it, the O'odham lacked proprietary control over the land. The major problem was that the reservation was open to mineral entry by anyone who wanted to file a claim. Miners made many claims—and abandoned many of them also, which sometimes benefited the O'odham.

The Emergency Conservation Work program was involved occasionally in improving water sources that miners had developed on

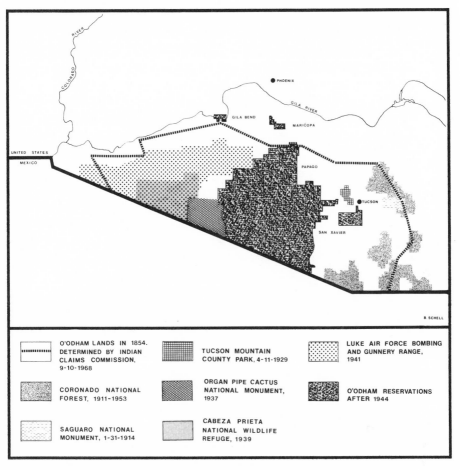

Legend:

- O'ODHAM LANDS IN 1854. DETERMINED BY INDIAN CLAIMS COMMISSION, 9-10-1968
- CORONADO NATIONAL FOREST, 1911-1953
- SAGUARO NATIONAL MONUMENT, 1-31-1914
- TUCSON MOUNTAIN COUNTY PARK, 4-11-1929
- ORGAN PIPE CACTUS NATIONAL MONUMENT, 1937
- CABEZA PRIETA NATIONAL WILDLIFE REFUGE, 1939
- LUKE AIR FORCE BOMBING AND GUNNERY RANGE, 1941
- O'ODHAM RESERVATIONS AFTER 1944

## O'odham lands reserved by the United States

their claims. If the miner left his claim and gave permission, the O'od-ham cattlemen could use the water. Also, the mines offered some employment to the O'odham, but during the Depression, fewer small mines were profitable.

In 1931, the superintendent of the reservation asked a U.S. district attorney to assist twelve O'odham workers who had not been paid by the El Oro Mining Company, which had suspended operations. The mining company owed each man between $111.00 and $201.00 for services performed, for a total of $1,941.30. The company president had allegedly guaranteed the wages, but he was in California. The

143

records do not indicate whether the men recovered their wages, but at that time of desperate financial problems, it is unlikely they did.

As time went on, the O'odham wanted more control over the land, and they pushed to have the rights to mineral entry by outsiders removed. In October 1932, the Interior Department closed the reservation to mineral entry, but the complaints were loud enough for Congress to hear. Among those opposed to closing the reservation to mining were many O'odham who feared jobs would be lost if the mines were shut down.

In June 1934, an act of Congress reopened the reservation for mineral exploration and exploitation, and in 1935, outsiders had 11,044 acres of reservation land under claim, including 3,444 acres for standard lode mines and 7,600 acres for placer operations. The O'odham could have filed claims, but apparently none did. However, there were no major finds on the reservation in the twentieth century, and the major mines were west and east of the reservation.

Developments continued in social services on the reservation. The hospital at Sells, built by the Indian Bureau in 1921, continued to provide health care to the O'odham who wanted it, although many still favored traditional medicine. Many others combined traditional and modern treatments.

The eye disease trachoma continued to be a problem. Eye disease was endemic to the Indians, who spent much of their time outside and still lived in houses with dirt floors and no glass in the windows. Trachoma reportedly was prevalent among the O'odham living in the Indian village near Tucson as well as on the reservation.

Tuberculosis was also endemic to the O'odham settlements, and a sanatorium at San Xavier was completed in 1932 to serve the O'odham in that district and in Tucson. Cost overruns raised some ire at the Indian Office, but the sanatorium remained.

Education continued to be a major interest on the reservation. The Indian Bureau and agency officials placed special emphasis on learning in schools, and they proposed new schools for the areas reclaimed by purchase and added to the reservation. Some children walked two or three miles to reach their schools. Others who lived farther away rode buses. Although most of the day schools taught only the first three grades, the schools at Sells and Santa Rosa offered education to the seventh grade.

Kerwo, in the southwestern part of the reservation, had resisted many programs and schools because of a bias toward traditional

Building a day school on the reservation, 1935 (Courtesy of Venito Garcia Library, Sells)

ways, but even Kerwo accepted a schoolteacher in 1935. The teacher built attendance from the 3 children who first attended to 47 students two years later, when another teacher was hired, and a temporary building was constructed. The Public Works Administration program provided some of the labor to erect the building.

Approximately 1,185 children from the reservation attended school in 1936. There were eight government day schools, in which 553 children were enrolled, and ten mission schools with 443 students. Non-reservation boarding schools attracted 105 students, usually in higher grades than most of the day schools offered. There were also 84 children enrolled in public schools such as those at Ajo. Still, some 200 O'odham school-aged children on and off the reservation had never enrolled in school.

Often, the school buildings were temporary or insufficient because equipment was in short supply, and the financial support did not cover much more than operating costs. There were not enough books and paper, and playground equipment was available at only one or two schools.

The schools offered more than instruction. They often supplied

**145**

lunches for the attending children. A doctor and three nurses handled the medical needs, but because the medical officials also had other responsibilities, teachers treated the skin and eye diseases that were diagnosed. The schools also offered health education, and changes in home sanitation, and the gradual acceptance of more modern houses, helped to improve health conditions.

The Catholic and the Presbyterian churches ran some of the reservation schools. The Catholics were still firmly entrenched in San Xavier and operated a school at the mission. They also opened numerous day schools on the main reservation. The Presbyterians operated a couple of schools on the main reservation, mostly in the southeastern part. The two churches zealously guarded what they considered their territory and people. Even the federal government found itself in squabbles with the churches over where it should locate schools, and which children should attend those schools.

The conflict between the Presbyterians and the Catholics had begun years before, however, early in the twentieth century, when the Presbyterians moved actively onto the O'odham lands. Catholics had monopolized the Christian religious activities of the region since Father Kino's time, so they did not welcome competition with a great deal of enthusiasm.

Presbyterianism found its greatest following among the students who returned from the boarding schools, where they had been exposed to new ideas and ways. In 1911, the Presbyterians had been instrumental in the formation of the Good Government League, which lobbied for the establishment of the main reservation, and they maintained a reputation as an activist group among the O'odham. They often favored innovations and new government programs.

The Catholics usually were oriented more toward the traditional practices. They backed the League of Papago Chiefs, which many Catholics helped organize in 1925. The group's main advisor was Father Bonaventure Oblasser, and many of the headmen, or village chiefs, were members. Although the group advocated a minimum of interference by the Indian agency in local affairs, its members were usually willing to accept as much federal assistance as possible for schools, water development, and health services.

Also on the reservation were people who professed to be Sonoran Catholic. This mixture of Catholicism and traditional Indian religion had developed among the native peoples who had received missionaries at one time, but then had lived without close supervision by priests.

Medicine man, San Xavier (Courtesy of Venito
Garcia Library, Sells)

The native people took what seemed to work for them from the Catholic teachings and combined those principles with native beliefs. The result was a religion that had many Catholic attributes but avoided the direction of the Catholic church and its priests.

The traditional practices of the O'odham were not as formalized as those of some other Indian groups, such as the Pueblo Indians. The religious activities were bound in the rituals of purification for hunting, menstruation, war, and salt pilgrimages.

Perhaps the most significant religious ritual was the rain-bringing ceremony, or *vi:gida,* which involved the making and drinking of tiswin, prepared from the saguaro cactus fruit. Healing practices of the medicine men also constituted a large part of the religious orientation. However, there was no formal religious institution or body of authorities that maintained a dogma or prescribed rules of conduct.

The people who retained most of the native traditions were usually those who had been least influenced by the encroaching culture. They were the farthest removed from the towns, the least willing to change their ways, and the last to be drawn into the educational system, which taught not only English and academic subjects but also the values of the dominant culture.

President Franklin D. Roosevelt's appointment of John Collier as the commissioner of Indian affairs presaged the coming of many changes for the Indian tribes. Collier pushed for the passage of the Wheeler-Howard Act of June 18, 1934, which is often called the Indian Reorganization Act. This act effectively ended the Dawes Severalty Act, or the General Allotment Act, of 1887, which had been an instrument to reduce Indian ownership of reservation land.

The Wheeler-Howard Act attempted to reverse the process by which Indians were losing their lands. No longer could Indian land be divided into individual parcels and be subject to sale by the owners. Although this had not been a problem for the O'odham, many tribes had lost much of what they had possessed prior to the allotting process.

The Collier administration also encouraged perpetuation of native religions and cultures. The Indians were to become bilingual rather than to speak only English at the expense of their native tongue.

Another provision of the Wheeler-Howard Act allowed the various tribes to create their own governments. Members of the individual tribes were to vote on whether they wanted to organize a tribal government or not, and if they chose to do so, they were to write constitutions and by-laws and submit them to the Indian Bureau for approval. After the bureau approved the constitutions, the tribes could determine their governments and install them according to the process detailed within those constitutions.

This was certainly an improvement over the previous system, which allowed the Indian Bureau considerable power over the affairs of Indian tribes. However, the system forced tribes to organize strong centralized governments to control the affairs of all tribal members. The O'odham had never really had any formal government beyond the realm of the village. The council of elders had made decisions on the village level. A person voted by voicing his opinions at the village council meetings, and everyone who attended knew how the others felt about the issues.

As the Wheeler-Howard Act progressed through Congress, an amendment was added that specifically required that the Papago Reservation be open for mineral entry. This one item caused considerable debate among the O'odham, who were not sure they should vote to accept reorganization under the act if it meant agreeing to allow mineral entry. The O'odham, through Father Oblasser, sent several letters soliciting opinions as to what effect the act would have regarding surface rights on the reservation. The answers indicated that any developed areas on the surface would be protected, and with that reassurance, the O'odham seemed to favor the idea of reorganization.

A December 15, 1934, referendum on the Wheeler-Howard Act showed overwhelming support for reorganization. The vote attracted 48 percent of the eligible voters on the three O'odham reservations, and of those, 88 percent favored accepting the act. More eligible women voted than men. The Kerwo precinct refused to vote because it required a secret ballot. They had always decided issues based on a public show of support or opposition, and they did not want to change for this issue.

During 1935, the O'odham and the agency decided to divide the reservation into eleven districts, which roughly followed the lines dividing the separate linguistic groups, as much as they still existed. The nine fenced grazing districts on the main reservation were each a district, and the San Xavier and Gila Bend reservations were the other two. A council of no fewer than five members was to govern each district, and each village was to have at least one representative. Representatives were to own at least five head of cattle because cattle raising was the principal industry on the reservation. After the district council was in place, it was to elect two more members from the district to represent the people who did not own cattle.

Then each district council was to elect a delegate and an alternate delegate to the Papago Council, which would be the governing organization of the tribe. It would select a chairman and other officers from its members.

In December 1935, a list of delegates for the constitutional convention included twenty-four names. Most districts listed two delegates, but two had only one each. There were also four delegates-at-large. The list changed several times before the convention assembled, but finally a group of O'odham men produced a suitable constitution for the tribe.

The superintendent sent a preliminary draft of the proposed constitution to the Indian Office on January 21, 1936, with a warning that one paragraph would probably not meet approval: the paragraph

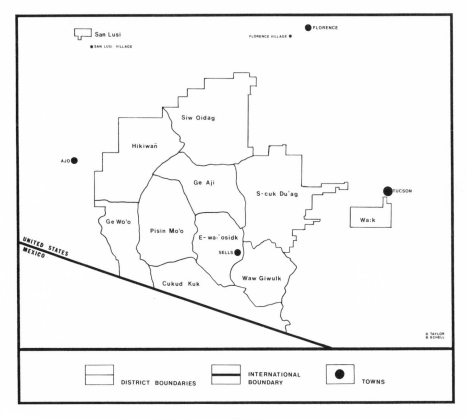

San Lusi

SAN LUSI VILLAGE

FLORENCE

FLORENCE VILLAGE

Siw Oidag

Hikiwañ

AJO

Ge Aji

S-cuk Du'ag

TUCSON

Ge Wo'o

Pisin Mo'o

E-wa:'osidk

Wa:k

UNITED STATES
MEXICO

SELLS

Cukud Kuk

Waw Giwulk

D TAYLOR
B SCHELL

DISTRICT BOUNDARIES

INTERNATIONAL
BOUNDARY

TOWNS

## Districts of the O'odham tribal government

stated that livestock owners should have the right to handle their stock as they wanted within their districts. The O'odham livestock raisers wanted to retain individual control over their businesses, but this appeared counter to one of the regulations of the Wheeler-Howard Act.

The tribe held a meeting on February 29, 1936, to discuss the proposed constitution and then vote to accept or reject it. Those who attended discussed the constitution section by section and voted whether changes needed to be made. After some debate, they rejected one section that would have withdrawn membership from the tribe of those who moved off the reservation.

The Papago Council held another meeting on April 18, 1936, to consider certain sections of the proposed constitution, but other than one revision to allow leasing of land to non-Indians, the constitution passed unchanged.

The chairman of the constitutional committee, Jose X. Pablo, and other committee members submitted the proposed constitution to Harold L. Ickes, secretary of the interior, on May 4, 1936. The work of the committee was finished, pending the review by the Indian Bureau and the Department of the Interior.

By July, the tribe had heard nothing from Washington, D.C., about the status of the constitution, and the superintendent recommended that the tribe elect a temporary council to function as the tribal government until the agencies ratified the constitution. The council actually consisted of the delegates involved with the creation of the constitution, and they also elected leaders from that group. Although Jose Ignacio did not vote for himself, he was named the chairman of the temporary council. John Ortiz was the vice chairman.

The secretary of the interior approved the constitution and by-laws on January 6, 1937, marking the first time in history that the Papago tribe had been unified under a single government. The eleven districts within the reservation, including San Xavier and Gila Bend, remained, as they do today, the political divisions of the reservations. They continue to have their own councils and chairmen, which function with some autonomy in district matters.

Jose Ignacio remained chairman of the tribe after approval made the tribal government official, and he held the post from 1937 to 1940, when Peter Blaine, Sr., succeeded him.

One major problem during the 1930s was the situation with the Mexican O'odham. By the treaties which brought half of the Papaguería to the United States, the O'odham were to have free access to cross the border. This was to ensure that the O'odham could maintain an identity as a people. Many Mexican O'odham spent parts of the year living in the United States, and many of the O'odham from the United States spent summers or other seasons in Mexico with relatives. Many others went for two or three weeks for various celebrations. Many O'odham living today recall having spent long periods of their youth in Mexico.

The O'odham in Mexico theoretically had more rights as citizens of Mexico than the O'odham in the United States, until 1924, when Indians in the United States were made citizens. Practically, however, they may have had fewer rights because much of their land was more attractive to ranchers and farmers than were the reservation lands in the United States.

The O'odham in Mexico did not know how to use the law to protect themselves, just as those in the United States had not understood how to use their laws in earlier times. The Mexican O'odham had been driven off their lands, and the Mexican government set aside for them only a few small reserves. They had nothing like the large reservation in the United States, and ranchers moved in and took the lands they had used to graze their livestock. Rights of prior use seemed to have no bearing on the situation, and the problem continues today.

The 1930s were a decade of suffering, learning, and great change for the O'odham. They ended the decade as an independent government within a government. However, the Indian Bureau still exerted considerable control over what they did because the superintendent and the Indian Bureau could still veto acts of their councils. Eventually such control would lessen, but it would never completely fade away. More changes were in store as the world around them changed, but challenges were a way of life for the O'odham, who had made the desert their home for untold years.

# 11

## Postwar Progress

*"Well, what God gives you, if you don't use, he will not give any*
*more. If you do not pick the saguaro fruit," she says, "you won't*
*have any more."*                    CLARA BONNIE PRICE, Interview

The years of war and the subsequent period of recovery were also
years of development and change for the O'odham. Many O'odham
developed skills and technical knowledge through involvement in the
work and relief programs of the New Deal, and they then found a
market for those skills during World War II.

Numerous O'odham left the reservation to take jobs in war industries and to replace workers who had left their jobs for other work or
to become soldiers. Some O'odham became soldiers, too. After the
war, changes in the economy and technological advances led to a dis-
location of some O'odham when their jobs, mostly those off the reservation, were eliminated. In the meantime, the tribe's government had
to continue to grow and learn how to be effective.

The relief programs of the Depression began to bring the entire
reservation into the cash economy that was prevalent in most of the
United States, and the O'odham were less inclined to barter or to
gather the wild foods than were their parents and grandparents. The
young O'odham had grown up earning wages for their work and
learning to spend those wages to procure food, clothing, and a variety
of other consumer goods.

While the older O'odham were happy to have the use of a wagon
for transportation, the younger generation began to desire automobiles and pickup trucks. Radios, and later televisions, provided entertainment, and these new consumer items also brought about cultural
changes.

Radio and television brought constant contact with the English language, which made learning that language much easier. The O'odham
language was useful only with other O'odham or their Pima cousins.

For commercial entertainment, education, business, and interaction with the federal government, English was a necessary tool. Spanish, the major second language for years, also became less useful.

With an automobile to travel the good roads, which had been constructed during the 1930s, the O'odham could easily travel to Tucson or Ajo, and they found jobs in construction, mining, and other industries. Because wages enabled them to buy food and consumer items, traditional ways of food procurement became less important, especially to the younger people. When they left the reservation to work, they did not receive their families' guidance, and no longer did young people learn skills of survival from extended family members.

Even the O'odham who stayed on the reservation were no longer dependent on each other, and the communal activities and sharing of food within a village played a less important role in their lives. The desert, which had for generations controlled them, had lost much of its power over them. In varying degrees, they joined in the pursuit of higher wages and increasing wealth, a characteristic learned from the majority of citizens of the United States as well as other parts of the world. Acquiring personal wealth had been foreign to the O'odham in earlier times.

During the Depression of the 1930s, a great number of people came from Oklahoma, Texas, Kansas, and Arkansas as migrant workers, and they competed with the Indians for work in the southern Arizona cotton fields. However, after World War II broke out in 1939, most of the non-Indian migrant workers left Arizona for California. There they found jobs in the war industries—or took over the work of people who had left to accept the higher-paying jobs in those industries. Even some of those who remained in Arizona changed jobs and moved to the cities of Tucson and Phoenix for war-related work.

Thus the cotton picking was left almost exclusively to the O'odham and Pimas, who were in great demand through the war years. All farm production during World War II was considered essential to the war effort, and the U.S. government conducted extensive campaigns asking people to work on the farms, raise gardens, and do everything possible to increase food and fiber production. Such campaigns led the O'odham to look upon their role in the cotton industry as a patriotic duty to help the nation during this great struggle.

The O'odham also contributed directly to the war effort. Some 250 young O'odham, nearly all men, served in the armed forces and fought in all the arenas of conflict. Eighteen O'odham died, and others were

O'odham worker plowing a cotton field (Courtesy of Venito Garcia Library, Sells)

wounded. They all experienced life far from the reservation, and many developed skills that would help them after the war. Some of the soldiers remained with the armed forces after the war ended, and many of them, along with new recruits, fought in Korea five years after World War II ended.

Most of those who served in the armed forces had been drafted, which gave rise to a troublesome episode. An older man named Pi Ha-Maccuda of the village near Hikiwañ was opposed not only to the draft but also to the Gadsden Purchase and the Indian Reorganization Act. He and his friend Leandro were worried about O'odham leaving to fight in a war about which the people knew very little. The federal government's reaction to these two old men was to send sheriffs to the village of S-tuha Bidag to arrest them. They were tried, found guilty, sentenced to long terms in the federal penitentiary for opposing the draft, and sent to Terminal Island, California, to serve their sentences. However, a couple of years later, when Pi Ha-Maccuda's daughter broke her arm, the tribal chairman, Peter Blaine, interceded with a judge and got them released.

The war experience had many sides and affected each person differently. Although war is never pretty, its side effects at times are beneficial, and the economic recovery caused by the war did help many people. The military experience itself helped some and hurt others.

For many decades, O'odham men and women had worked in the mines on or surrounding their reservation. With copper being one of the strategic metals needed for the Allied war effort, increasing numbers of O'odham found work at Ajo and the other mines. The copper mines near Tucson also expanded. People employed in mining tended to receive higher wages than those who worked in cotton fields, but cotton picking was still an extremely important part of the O'odham economy.

Other O'odham found work outside the mining and cotton industries. Some left to work in airplane factories or in other war industries. Some went as far as Los Angeles to work in the shipyards. Another large group worked on the railroads, maintaining ballast and repairing bridges and trestles. This was one of the most important jobs during World War II because the transportation network was crucial to conduct the war in the Pacific. The most reliable all-weather railroad route was, of course, the southern route, which ran near the northern edge of the O'odham reservations.

One of the areas of O'odham employment that seemed to shift during World War II was domestic service. Young women had found work in domestic service, especially in Tucson, for generations, but the demand for servants declined during and after the war. It was more patriotic to use all available labor in war industries to help assure victory for the Allies.

On the reservation, the mainstay of the O'odham economy was still the cattle industry. During the 1930s, a cattlemen's association was organized to unify the owners in the direction their industry should go. However, the number of cattle on the reservation remained large, larger than the federal government thought was advisable for the reservation's range, and the reduction of the size of the herds became a source of contention between the Bureau of Indian Affairs and Peter Blaine while he was tribal chairman. Blaine thought the O'odham should make the decisions regarding the number of cattle allowed on the reservation.

The cattle industry benefited greatly from the increased prices that resulted during the worldwide food shortage of the 1940s. The price of cattle roughly doubled during the war, and the price of cattle sold from the reservation rose dramatically. In September 1945, reports from the Bureau of Indian Affairs indicate that the average price for a cow was $54.00, while steers sold for $48.00, heifers and bulls for $46.00, and calves for $34.00. It should be noted that this was not pure increase in income to the O'odham because there was some inflation that devalued the money.

Despite inflation, the price of cattle rose more than the cost of other goods. For instance, in 1942, O'odham livestock producers sold 961 head of cattle, at an average price per head of $33.71. In 1945, they sold 818 head at an average price of $43.50, an increase of almost $10.00 per head in three years.

The success of the cattle industry during the war led to the start of a tribal cattle herd as a means of raising revenue, but the tribal council also imposed a reservation grazing fee to earn money and to better control the number of cattle on the range.

Income from horses on the reservation rose also, but not because of the regular market factors. A serious infection called dourine, a disease carried by horses imported from Great Britain, broke out among the horse herds and spread rapidly on the reservation. Many of the owners sold the infected animals, and as was the case with the scrub ponies of earlier periods, dog-food factories purchased most of them.

Horsehides were worth money, too. During 1942, the records indicate the sale of only one horse. In 1943, the O'odham sold 148 horses at $11.28 per horse. Although $11.00 per animal was not a great price, it was not unusual to sell diseased horses at that low rate. This price was just about the market value of that time for horses bought for dog food and for use by animal by-products companies to make glues or fertilizers. In 1944, tribal members sold 544 animals at an average price of $10.23. In part, this represented the determination of both the horse owners and the Bureau of Indian Affairs to rid the reservation of dourine.

Another wartime event in Tohono O'odham country was the establishment of an air force base near Phoenix, which required the creation of a gunnery range for practice bombing runs and tests of experimental weapons. The government established the gunnery range on the northern and western flanks of the O'odham Reservation, and although the United States did not take any reservation territory, the range consisted mostly of traditional O'odham lands. The range was huge, stretching from roughly the upper reaches of Kohatk Wash near Freeman, Arizona, and west nearly to Yuma, a distance of nearly two hundred miles.

An agreement was worked out between the Tohono O'odham Tribal Council and the U.S. government over the use of the area, known as the Air Force Base Gunnery Range and later called the Luke Air Force Range. More recently, the range has been renamed again, and it is now officially called the Barry M. Goldwater Air Force Gunnery Range.

The O'odham realized the necessity of having a practice range for the training of pilots for war, and they agreed to allow some use of their lands, including some emergency landing strips on the reservation itself. They also witnessed the construction of Ryan Field, west of Tucson, on traditional O'odham lands.

The tribal council also approved overflights of the reservation, and Henry Throssell, one of the prominent leaders on the council and chairman from 1943 to 1944, was particularly in favor of allowing flights in the area. His son was in training to become a pilot for the army air corps, and he apparently landed on reservation roads several times. Unfortunately, he died in a crash before completing the training.

The approval by the council did not specify any time period for the overflights, and the army, and later the air force, assumed the approval was for as long as they wanted to fly over the reservation. However, problems arose when jet training began to create noise pollution and sonic booms. In the late 1970s, the air force began an environmental impact study to determine whether the overflights had detrimental effects on the reservation, but the study was never completed. The overflights continued into the 1990s despite years of protest by the O'odham.

The major effect of the air force range was to prohibit any remaining use of this land by the Hia C'eḍ O'odham, who had traditionally used most of this region. Creation of the gunnery range, coupled with the loss of Organ Pipe Cactus National Monument and the Cabeza Prieta Game Refuge, left virtually no traditional lands within the United States for the Hia C'eḍ O'odham.

As World War II began, the O'odham were just becoming acquainted with self-government. As mentioned previously, the tribe had created a government in 1937 under the Indian Reorganization Act, and the first tribal chairman was Jose Ignacio. The second chairman was Peter Blaine, and much more is known about his administra-

Henry Throssell (*left, holding camera*) and other members of the Papago
Rodeo and Fair Association, 1940s: *next right,* Manuel Puella; *center, gray
hat,* Richard Hendricks; *next right, black hat,* Peter Blaine; *next right, front
row,* Juan Harvey. (Courtesy of Venito Garcia Library, Sells)

tion because of his substantial memoirs, *Papagos and Politics,* a book
jointly authored with Michael S. Adams and published by the Arizona
Historical Society in 1981.

The chairman of the Papago Council served a one-year term, but
the O'odham generally retained the chairman for more than one term.
Many served for four or more terms before retiring or losing to another candidate. At first, the Papago Tribal Council was responsible
for the selection of the chairman. A later change in the constitution led
to direct election of the chairman by all voters.

In the late 1950s, another change was proposed. A one-year term
hardly allows a person to become familiar with his job before he must
think of reelection, and the proposed change would have allowed for
some continuity in the leadership by extending the chairman's term to
four years.

**159**

Council members also proposed that the tribe be allowed to enter into mineral leases, and to have the authority to use the money received from that source. Under the old system, the money received from leases went to the federal treasury, from which it was allocated back to the tribe. The proponents of the constitutional change wanted to eliminate the control the Treasury Department might try to have over the use of such funds.

The O'odham voted on the proposed changes in May 1958. Although not all of the districts voted on the same day, on May 17, the election results showed that eight of the eleven districts opposed the changes to the constitution. It was not until the 1980s that the tribe's voters ratified a new constitution, and it included a provision extending the chairman's term to four years.

World War II ended in 1945, but unlike the first world war, the end of the second did not bring a depression. There was a steady demand for cotton, which in turn created a demand for workers, and the O'odham continued to be the most reliable source of labor available to the cotton growers until mechanization drastically reduced the demands for human labor.

At the end of the war, the O'odham elected Thomas Segundo to be the tribal chairman. Segundo was a hard-working young man who was active on and off the reservation trying to improve conditions for the O'odham. He spoke English very well, which made working with national government leaders easy for him, and he served six consecutive terms, ably championing the interests of the O'odham and their reservation.

In 1948, under Segundo's leadership and with the cooperation of the Department of the Interior, the Papago Tribal Council compiled the Papago Development Program. This report proposed to Congress that aid be given for irrigation projects, range improvement, charco farming, education, health, roads, telephone systems, credit, social security, community facilities, and relocation for individuals who wanted to leave the reservation. Although Congress never approved this program, the tribal government successfully implemented parts of it between 1953 and 1958.

Segundo left the reservation after his first six terms to pursue opportunities off the reservation, including education at the University of Chicago. He later returned, and in 1967, he was again elected chairman. Segundo continued to lead new programs on the reserva-

Thomas Segundo, tribal chairman, 1947–1953 and
1968–1971 (Courtesy of Venito Garcia Library, Sells)

tion until he died in an airplane crash en route to speak to a group of
O'odham and other Native Americans attending college in the eastern
United States. The plane from Tucson crashed outside Phoenix on
May 6, 1971.

One of the O'odham's major complaints had been taken care of in
May 1955 when an act of Congress returned full rights to the minerals of their lands. The tribe could require permits for prospecting and
royalties from any ores taken from the reservation. Even though no
large discoveries of important ores have been found on the reservation
since that time, people can no longer enter the reservation at their
pleasure and search for promising mineral deposits, nor can they stake
claims and eliminate areas from use by the O'odham.

In the San Xavier district, the American Smelting & Refining Company had bid $1,066,007 for the right to prospect there, and ex-
ploration had begun in 1954. After drilling 346 holes, the company
determined that there was enough high-grade copper ore to be worth
extracting. In May 1957, the company paid for permission to
prospect 15,432 acres. The Papago Tribe owned only 160 acres, for
which it received $24,000. The remainder belonged to heirs of allot-

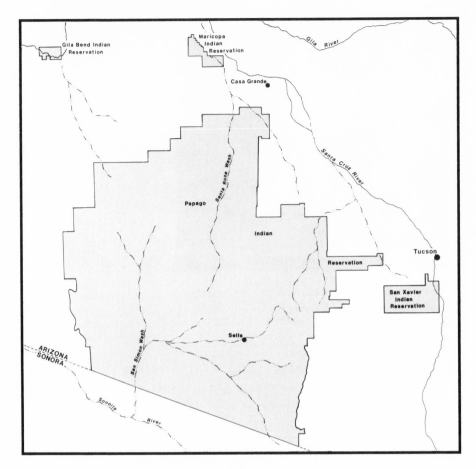

## Tohono O'odham lands, 1956

tees, and individual O'odham from San Xavier received from $.30 to $30,000 for the use of their land, plus the promise of royalties for all ore removed from the site.

The first payments went to the tribe, which were then distributed to the individual owners. Some owners received lump-sum payments, while others had their funds placed in accounts from which they received small periodic payments. People who received substantial amounts of money used it in various ways: some bought cars or trucks, some improved their houses, and some dug wells and purchased tractors. At last, some of the O'odham finally benefited from the minerals found on their lands.

On August 13, 1946, Congress created the Indian Claims Commission to evaluate claims of Indian groups who believed the United States had not treated them fairly and honorably. Many treaties that the United States had made with Indian tribes had been ignored, violated, and forgotten, and although the commission could not return land, it could compensate tribes with monetary settlements.

Even though the O'odham had never had a treaty with the United States, they filed a petition contesting that the federal government had failed to protect their lands. Besides the claim of aboriginal use, the O'odham could use the treaties with Mexico that stipulated that they should have rights to their lands. For several years, scholars and lawyers wrote reports, talked to witnesses, and searched archives for materials to support the O'odham claims, and these activities not only helped win a favorable decision (finally made September 10, 1968), but they also added much to the knowledge of the O'odham, their history, and their land.

The commission's findings that the O'odham had aboriginal title to the land called the Papaguería opened the door for a cash settlement, but it took another eight years for both parties to agree on the sum of $26 million for the lost lands. Of course, the lands in Mexico, which were at least half of the O'odham lands when the first Europeans moved into the area, were lost forever, and the U.S. government could make no compensation for them. Much of the land in Mexico that remains in O'odham control continues to be in jeopardy.

Another land issue involved the construction on Kitt Peak of what at that time was the world's largest astronomical observatory. Kitt Peak was a sacred mountain to the Tohono O'odham, second only to Baboquivari Peak in significance. However, the people involved in selecting the observatory site considered the Kitt Peak location to be the best site. The dry desert air, the lack of pollution, the distance from a major city, and the proximity to the University of Arizona all added to its attraction.

Eventually, the O'odham agreed to lease the land at the summit of the mountain for the construction of the telescopes, and the building of the observatory created jobs for the O'odham. Construction jobs were temporary, but some maintenance work was permanent. The builders finished the first stages of the observatory in 1959.

At the end of 1960, the O'odham became involved in another quarrel with the federal government. The U.S. Army Corps of Engineers planned to build a flood-control dam on the Gila River near Gila

Bend, but before construction began, the engineers determined that the homes of twenty O'odham families located in the basin could be flooded if the dam were to back water up to its capacity. Statistically, this was liable to happen once every fifty-six years.

The government promised the O'odham that it would relocate their village, the old village called Si:l Mekk, to higher ground at the government's expense, and further promised the tribe $130,000 for a flowage easement on reservation lands subject to flooding by the dam. However, after completion of the dam and neglect of all the promises, the O'odham asked when they could expect the new houses and money, and they were told that the Army Corps of Engineers had learned that Si:l Mekk did not lie within the boundaries of the Gila Bend Reservation. The families were squatters and could not prove ownership of the land, and they could not receive compensation for land they did not own. Moreover, the houses that they had requested would cost far more than the simple huts and shacks that they had to leave.

The O'odham replied that Si:l Mekk had been the main village of the Gila Bend Reservation until President Taft reduced the size of the reserve and left that village outside the boundaries. The O'odham therefore had rights of continuous occupation since at least 1882. Moreover, when the engineers had offered to move them, they had asked the families what kind of housing they would like and suggested a style used at Sells. The families had accepted that style and expected the engineers to build those houses.

Disputes about land were not the only difficulties confronting the O'odham. Water continued to be a problem in the Southwestern desert country. The government and the tribe spent more than $1 million during the 1950s to develop water on the reservation, but water development for the reservation was not the only issue. The city of Tucson's rapid growth necessitated that new sources of water be found, and the city drilled new wells near the San Xavier District boundaries and in the Avra and Altar valleys.

The O'odham blamed the drilling of these wells for the loss of water at San Xavier and also on the main reservation. San Xavier lost all water from shallow wells that the residents had used for many generations. In April 1967, the O'odham filed suit to stop Tucson from operating nine wells that supplied the city with almost seven million gallons of water each day. The issue remained in court for years, but the tribe eventually won.

O'odham family and their ramada, San Xavier (Courtesy of Venito Garcia Library, Sells)

By the late 1960s, the O'odham did almost no farming on the San Xavier lands because of the lack of water. What will happen with the allotment of Central Arizona Project water has yet to be determined, but large-scale farming could never develop because other people had taken over or destroyed the old water sources that had kept San Xavier green for centuries.

In the late 1970s, the O'odham filed another suit against the city of Tucson and some 1,750 miners, farmers, and other water users to protect the water rights of the O'odham. On October 11, 1983, when Josiah Moore was tribal chairman, the Southern Arizona Water Rights Settlement Act settled the issue, promising the O'odham water rights and money to settle claims for lost water.

Not every event involved disagreement with the local or national governments. When the old hospital in Sells burned down in 1947, the sanatorium at San Xavier temporarily became the reservation hospital, but on July 25, 1959, officials broke ground at Sells for construction of a $1.4 million hospital. The same day, a new clinic at Santa

**165**

Rosa was dedicated. Upon completion of the hospital in 1961, the sanatorium at San Xavier again became the convalescence center for tuberculosis victims.

Education continued to be important, but the O'odham were not wealthy enough to develop schooling through the higher grades until the 1970s. There are some high schools on the reservation now, and many O'odham aspire to and acquire college educations.

In some of the schools, bilingual instruction is available, and that should help ease the pressure that English is exerting on the reservation. The O'odham realize that their language is a major part of their heritage and culture, and that for the language to continue being useful, it must be taught in the homes and in the schools.

Also in the 1970s and 1980s came pressure from the federal government to restrict access to the border with Mexico because of the threat of drug trafficking. Drug dealers have tried to recruit the O'odham to transport drugs because of the freedom they have to cross the international border, and some of them have exerted pressure on the O'odham in Mexico as they buy ranches and other lands along the border, areas that the O'odham have used for grazing or that contain sacred places or shrines.

The pressures of change and encroachment never seem to relent as they push the O'odham. The physical and cultural forms of these pressures, as well as their intensity, may vary, but the pressure is unending.

The O'odham have become assimilated into United States culture to some degree. They possess automobiles, trucks, telephones, televisions, and many of the amenities that modern technology offers, and often these things form their values. Many O'odham have become well educated and have left the reservation to take advantage of economic and professional activities that are not available there.

However, many who leave the reservation yearn to return to help in the development of the people and of their ancestral home. Their desert land is special. It is where their ancestors were able to adapt to the land and make it work for them. It is where the O'odham can continue to change as needed, yet maintain their distinctive identity and share their traditions.

# Selected Bibliography

BOOKS

Bahr, Donald M. *Pima and Papago Ritual Oratory: A Study of Three Texts.* San Francisco: The Indian Historian Press, 1975.

Bancroft, Hubert Howe. *History of the North Mexican States and Texas.* Vol. I, 1531–1800, vol. II, 1801–1889. San Francisco: The History Company, Publishers, 1889.

Bannon, John Francis. *The Spanish Borderlands Frontier, 1513–1821.* Albuquerque: University of New Mexico Press, 1974.

Bartlett, Richard A. *Great Surveys of the American West.* Norman: University of Oklahoma Press, 1962.

Bazant, Jan. *A Concise History of Mexico from Hidalgo to Cárdenas, 1805–1940.* Cambridge: Cambridge University Press, 1977.

Beers, Henry Putney. *Spanish and Mexican Records of the American Southwest: A Bibliographical Guide to Archive and Manuscript Sources.* Tucson: The University of Arizona Press, 1979.

Blaine, Peter. *Papagos and Politics.* Tucson: The Arizona Historical Society, 1981.

Bolton, Herbert Eugene. *The Padre on Horseback.* Chicago: Loyola University Press, 1963.

———. *Rim of Christendom: A Biography of Eusebio Francisco Kino, Pacific Coast Pioneer.* New York: Macmillan, 1936.

———, ed. *Spanish Exploration in the Southwest, 1542–1706.* New York: Barnes & Noble, 1967.

Bolton, Herbert Eugene, and Thomas Maitland Marshall. *The Colonization of North America, 1492–1783.* New York: Macmillan, 1960.

Bowman, J. N., and Robert F. Heizer. *Anza and the Northwest Frontier of New Spain.* Southwest Museum Papers, no. 20. Highland Park, Los Angeles: Southwest Museum, 1967.

Brown, F. Lee, and Helen M. Ingram. *Water and Poverty in the Southwest.* Tucson: The University of Arizona Press, 1987.

Bryan, Kirk. *The Papago Country, Arizona: A Geographic, Geologic, and Hydrologic Reconnaissance with a Guide to Desert Watering Places.* U.S.G.S. Water Supply Paper, no. 499. Washington, D.C.: GPO, 1925.

Castetter, Edward F., and Willis H. Bell. *Pima and Papago Indian Agriculture.* Albuquerque: University of New Mexico Press, 1942.

Cortés, José. *Views from the Apache Frontier: Report on the Northern Provinces of New Spain.* Edited by Elizabeth A. H. John and translated by John Wheat. Norman: University of Oklahoma Press, 1989.

Dobyns, Henry F. *The Papago People.* Phoenix: Indian Tribal Series, 1972.

Dunbier, Roger. *The Sonoran Desert: Its Geography, Economy, and People.* Tucson: The University of Arizona Press, 1968.

Elliott, Wallace W. *History of Arizona Territory Showing Its Resources and Advantages, 1884.* Flagstaff, Arizona: Northland Press, 1964.

Fontana, Bernard L. *Of Earth and Little Rain: The Papago Indians.* Flagstaff, Arizona: Northland Press, 1981.

———. "The Papago Tribe of Arizona." In vol. 3, *Papago Indians.* Indian Claims Commission Findings. New York: Garland Publishing, 1974.

Forbes, Jack D. *The Papago-Apache Treaty of 1853: Property Rights and Religious Liberties of the 'O'odham, Maricopa, and Other Native Peoples.* Davis, California: Native American Studies Tecumseh Center, University of California, Davis, 1979.

Gabel, Norman E. *A Comparative Racial Study of the Papago.* University of New Mexico Publications in Anthropology, no. 4. Albuquerque: University of New Mexico Press, 1949.

Gerhard, Peter. *The North Frontier of New Spain.* Princeton: Princeton University Press, 1982.

Gibson, Arrell Morgan. *The American Indian: Prehistory to the Present.* Lexington, Mass.: D. C. Heath and Company, 1980.

Goetzmann, William H. *Army Exploration in the American West, 1803–1863.* Lincoln: University of Nebraska Press, 1959.

*Greater America: Essays in Honor of Herbert Eugene Bolton.* Berkeley: University of California Press, 1945.

Hackenburg, Robert A. "Aboriginal Land Use and Occupancy of the Papago Indians." In vol. 1, *Papago Indians*. Indian Claims Commission Findings. New York: Garland Publishing Inc., 1974.

Hornaday, William T. *Camp-Fires on Desert and Lava*. New York: Charles Scribner's Sons, 1908.

Joseph, Alice, Rosamond B. Spicer, and Jane Chesky. *The Desert People: A Study of the Papago Indians*. Chicago: University of Chicago Press, 1949.

Kelly, William H. "The Papago Indians of Arizona." In vol. 3, *Papago Indians*. Indian Claims Commission Findings. New York: Garland Publishing Inc., 1974.

Kessell, John. *Friars, Soldiers, and Reformers*. Tucson: The University of Arizona Press, 1976.

————. *Mission of Sorrows: Jesuit Guevavi and the Pimas, 1691–1767*. Tucson: The University of Arizona Press, 1970.

King, William S., and Delmos J. Jones. "Papago Population Studies." Vol. 2, *Papago Indians*. Indian Claims Commission Findings. New York: Garland Publishing Inc., 1974.

Kino, Eusebio Francisco, S.J. *Kino's Plan for the Development of Pimería Alta, Arizona and Upper California: A Report to the Mexican Viceroy*. Translated and annotated by Ernest J. Burrus, S.J. Tucson: Arizona Pioneer's Historical Society, 1961.

Lopez-Manuel, Rosilda. *Tohono O'odham Education Standards, October, 1987*. Sells, Arizona: Tohono O'odham Education Department, 1987.

Lumholtz, Carl. *New Trails in Mexico: An Account of One Year's Exploration in North-Western Sonora, Mexico, and South-Western Arizona, 1909–1910*. New York: Charles Scribner's Sons, 1912.

Melham, Tom. "Rocky Vistas and Wild Valleys: North America's Great Basin, Sonoran, Mojave, and Chihuahuan." In *The Desert Realm: Lands of Majesty and Mystery*. Washington, D.C.: National Geographic Society, 1982.

Miller, Tom, ed. *Arizona: The Land and the People*. Tucson: The University of Arizona Press, 1986.

Moorhead, Max L. *The Presidio: Bastion of the Spanish Borderlands*. Norman: University of Oklahoma Press, 1975.

Nabhan, Gary Paul. *The Desert Smells Like Rain: A Naturalist in Papago Indian Country*. San Francisco: North Point Press, 1982.

Och, Joseph, S.J. *Missionary in Sonora: The Travel Reports of Joseph Och, S.J., 1755–1767*. Translated and annotated by Theodore E. Treutlein. San Francisco: California Historical Society, 1965.

Officer, James E. *Hispanic America, 1536–1856*. Tucson: The University of Arizona Press, 1987.

Pfefferkorn, Ignaz. *Sonora: A Description of the Province.* Translated and annotated by Theodore E. Treutlein. Albuquerque: University of New Mexico Press, 1949.

Poe, Charlsie. *Angel to the Papagos.* San Antonio, Texas: The Naylor Company, 1964.

Polzer, Charles W., S.J. *Kino Guide II: A Life of Eusebio Francisco Kino, S.J., Arizona's First Pioneer, and a Guide to His Missions and Monuments.* Tucson: Southwestern Mission Research Center, 1982.

Roca, Paul M. *Paths of the Padres through Sonora: An Illustrated History and Guide to Its Spanish Churches.* Tucson: Arizona Pioneer's Historical Society, 1967.

Sierra Club. *Saguaro We Going? Impacts of Population Growth in Eastern Pima County, Arizona.* Tucson: Sierra Club, Rincon Group, 1988.

Spicer, Edward H. *Cycles of Conquest: The Impact of Spain, Mexico, and the United States on the Indians of the Southwest, 1533–1960.* Tucson: The University of Arizona Press, 1962.

Tatom, William M., ed. *The Papago Indian Reservation and the Papago People.* Sells, Arizona: The Papago Tribe, 1975.

Tohono O'odham Tribe. *Tohono O'odham: History of the Desert People.* Sells, Arizona: Tohono O'odham Tribal Education Department, 1985.

———. *Tohono O'odham: Lives of the Desert People.* Sells, Arizona: Tohono O'odham Tribal Education Department, 1984.

Underhill, Ruth M. "Acculturation at the Papago Village of Santa Rosa." In vol. 1, *Papago Indians.* Indian Claims Commission Findings. New York: Garland Publishing Inc., 1974.

———. *A Papago Calendar Record.* The University of New Mexico Bulletin, no. 322. Albuquerque: University of New Mexico Press, 1938.

———. *Papago Woman.* New York: Holt, Rinehart and Winston, 1979.

———. *People of the Crimson Evening.* Palmer Lake, Colorado: The Filter Press, 1982.

———. *Singing for Power: The Song Magic of the Papago Indians of Southern Arizona.* New York: Ballantine Books, 1973.

———. *Social Organization of the Papago Indians.* New York: Columbia University Press, 1939.

Voss, Stuart F. *On the Periphery of Nineteenth-Century Mexico: Sonora and Sinaloa, 1810–1877.* Tucson: The University of Arizona Press, 1982.

Waddell, Jack O. *Papago Indians at Work.* Anthropological Papers of the University of Arizona, no. 12. Tucson: The University of Arizona Press, 1969.

Wagoner, Jay J. *Early Arizona: Prehistory to Civil War.* Tucson: The University of Arizona Press, 1975.

————. *History of the Cattle Industry in Southern Arizona, 1540–1940.* Social Science Bulletin, no. 20. Tucson: University of Arizona, 1952.

Walker, Henry P., and Don Bufkin. *Historical Atlas of Arizona.* Norman: University of Oklahoma Press, 1979.

Weber, David J. *The Mexican Frontier, 1821–1846: The American Southwest Under Mexico.* Albuquerque: University of New Mexico Press, 1982.

————. *The Taos Trappers: The Fur Trade in the Far Southwest, 1540–1846.* Norman: University of Oklahoma Press, 1970.

Wild, Peter. *The Saguaro Forest.* Photographs by Hal Coss. Flagstaff, Arizona: Northland Press, 1986.

Wilgus, A. Curtis, ed. *Colonial Hispanic America.* Washington, D.C.: George Washington University Press, 1936.

Xavier, Gwyneth N. "The Cattle Industry of the Southern Papago Districts." In vol. 1, *Papago Indians.* Indian Claims Commission Findings. New York: Garland Publishing Inc., 1974.

ARTICLES

Ahlborn, Richard E. "An Arizona Mission Font: Research Note to Fontana's 'Santa Ana de Cuiquiburitac.'" *Journal of the Southwest,* vol. 29 (summer 1987).

Anderson, Keith M., Fillman Bell, and Yvonne G. Stewart. "Quitobaquito: A Sand Papago Cemetery." *The Kiva,* vol. 47, no. 4 (1982).

Ayres, James E. "The Anglo Period in Archaeological and Historical Perspective." *The Kiva,* vol. 49, nos. 3–4 (1984).

Barnes, Mark R. "Hispanic Period Archaeology in the Tucson Basin: An Overview." *The Kiva,* vol. 49, nos. 3–4 (1984).

Brinckerhoff, Sidney B. "The Last Years of Spanish Arizona 1786–1821." *Arizona and the West,* vol. 9 (spring 1967).

Chesky, Jane. "The Wiikita." *The Kiva,* vol. 8 (Nov. 1942).

Cook, Charles A. "The Hunter Claim: A Colossal Land Scheme in the Papagueria." *Arizona and the West,* vol. 15 (autumn 1973).

Dobyns, Henry F. "Indian Extinction in the Middle Santa Cruz River Valley, Arizona." *New Mexico Historical Review,* vol. XXXVIII (Apr. 1963).

————. "Military Transculturation of Northern Piman Indians, 1782–1821." *Ethnohistory,* vol. 19 (fall 1972).

————. "A Papago Victory in 1854." *The Kiva,* vol. 23 (Oct. 1957).

Doelle, William H. "The Tucson Basin During the Protohistoric Period." *The Kiva,* vol. 49, nos. 3–4 (1984).

Ewing, Russell C. "The Pima Outbreak in November, 1751." *New Mexico Historical Review,* vol. XIII (Oct. 1938).

Ezell, Paul H. "Indians under the Law: Mexico, 1821–1847." *América Indígena*, vol. XV (July 1955).

Fontana, Bernard L. "The Papagos." *Arizona Highways*, vol. 59 (Apr. 1983).

———. "Santa Ana de Cuiquiburitac: Pimería Alta's Northernmost Mission." *Journal of the Southwest*, vol. 29 (summer 1987).

———. "Solar Power in the Land of the Papago." *Arizona Highways*, vol. 59 (Apr. 1983).

———. "The Unsolved Riddle of the River Hohokam." *Arizona Highways*, vol. 59 (Apr. 1983).

Forbes, Jack D. "Historical Survey of the Indians of Sonora, 1821–1910." *Ethnohistory*, vol. 4 (fall 1957).

Hammond, George P. "Pimería Alta after Kino's Time." *New Mexico Historical Review*, vol. IV (July 1929).

Hastings, James Rodney. "People of Reason and Others: The Colonization of Sonora to 1767." *Arizona and the West*, vol. 3 (winter 1961).

———. "The Tragedy at Camp Grant." *Arizona and the West*, vol. I (summer 1959).

Hendrix, Richard. "Talk by Richard Hendrix, Prominent Papago Indian, Given at the Arizona Archaeological and Historical Society, November 16, 1942." *The Kiva*, vol. 8 (Nov. 1942).

Herring, Patricia R. "A Plan for the Colonization of Sonora's Northern Frontier: The Paredes *Proyectos* of 1850." *The Journal of Arizona History*, vol. 10 (summer 1969).

Hill, W. W. "Notes of Pima Land Law and Tenure." *American Anthropologist*, New Series, vol. 38 (Oct.–Dec. 1936).

Hoover, J. W. "Generic Descent of the Papago Villages." *American Anthropologist*, New Series, vol. 37 (Apr.–June 1935).

Ives, Ronald L. "Population of the Pinacate Region, 1698–1706." *The Kiva*, vol. 31 (Oct. 1965).

Jackson, Robert H. "Causes of Indian Population Decline in the Pimería Alta Missions of Northern Sonora." *The Journal of Arizona History*, vol. 24 (winter 1983).

———. "The Last Jesuit Censuses of the Pimería Alta Missions, 1761 and 1766." *The Kiva*, vol. 46, no. 4 (1981).

Jones, Delmos J. "A Description of Settlement Pattern and Population Movement on the Papago Reservation." *The Kiva*, vol. 27 (Apr. 1962).

Kessell, John L. "Friars versus Bureaucrats: The Mission as a Threatened Institution on the Arizona-Sonora Frontier, 1767–1842." *The Western Historical Quarterly*, vol. V (Apr. 1974).

Lavender, David. "The Monuments and Memorials of the Gadsden Purchase." *Arizona Highways,* vol. 59 (Apr. 1983).

Mattison, Ray H. "Early Spanish and Mexican Settlements in Arizona." *New Mexico Historical Review,* vol. XXI (Oct., 1946).

———. "The Tangled Web: The Controversy Over the Tumacácori and Baca Land Grants." *The Journal of Arizona History,* vol. 8 (summer 1967).

Morrisey, Richard J. "Early Agriculture in Pimería Alta." *Mid-America: An Historical Review,* vol. 31, New Series, vol. 20 (Apr. 1949).

Park, Joseph F. "The Apaches in Mexican-American Relations, 1841–1861: A Footnote to the Gadsden Treaty." *Arizona and the West,* vol. 3 (summer 1961).

———. "Spanish Indian Policy in Northern Mexico, 1765–1810." *Arizona and the West,* vol. 4 (winter 1962).

Perschl, Nicholas. "Reminiscences of a Franciscan in Papagueria." *The Kiva,* vol. 24 (Feb. 1959).

Radding de Murrieta, Cynthia. "The Function of the Market in Changing Economic Structures in the Mission Communities of Pimeria Alta, 1768–1821." *The Americas,* vol. XXXIV (Oct. 1977).

Rippy, J. Fred. "The Indians of the Southwest in the Diplomacy of the United States and Mexico, 1848–1853." *The Hispanic American Historical Review,* vol. II (Aug. 1919).

Schmidt, Louis Bernard. "Manifest Opportunity and the Gadsden Purchase." *Arizona and the West,* vol. 3 (autumn 1961).

Smith, Dean. "The Gadsden Purchase 1983." *Arizona Highways,* vol. 59 (Apr. 1983).

———. "General Gadsden's Purchase." *Arizona Highways,* vol. 59, (Apr. 1983).

Smith, Ralph A. "Indians in American-Mexican Relations Before the War of 1846." *Hispanic American Historical Review,* vol. XLIII (Feb. 1963).

Spicer, Edward H. "European Expansion and the Enclavement of Southwestern Indians." *Arizona and the West,* vol. I (summer 1959).

Stevens, Robert C. "The Apache Menace in Sonora, 1831–1849." *Arizona and the West,* vol. 6 (autumn 1964).

Trimble, Marshall. "The Gadsden Purchase Survey—From Los Nogales, to Fort Yuma, along El Camino del Diablo." *Arizona Highways,* vol. 59 (Apr. 1983).

Whiting, Alfred F. "The Tumacacori Census of 1796." *The Kiva,* vol. 19 (fall 1953).

UNPUBLISHED WORKS

Adams, Michael L. "Every Stick and Stone: A History of the Papago People." Unpublished manuscript, revised under direction of Indian Oasis School District, 1978.

Barnett, George S. "Report Regarding the Tohono and Hia- Ced O'odham of Mexico Indigenous Peoples' Loss of Their Land, Violations of Convention 107 of the ILO, Violations of Treaty Rights, and the Lack of Protection for Cultural and Religious Rights of the O'Odham of Mexico and the United States." Photocopied manuscript, 1989.

Fontana, Bernard L. "Assimilative Change: A Papago Case Study." Ph.D. diss., University of Arizona, 1960.

————. "The Papago Indians," parts 1–3. Printed privately by Title IV, Indian Oasis School District 40, Sells, Arizona, 1976.

Fraga, Mike. "Indians in Mexico–United States Relations." Unpublished manuscript, 1979.

Lewis, David Rich. "Plowing a Civilized Furrow: Subsistence, Environment, and Social Change among the Northern Ute, Hupa, and Papago Peoples." Ph.D. diss. University of Wisconsin–Madison, 1988.

McCool, Daniel. "Federal Indian Policy and the Sacred Mountain of the Papago Indians." Paper presented at the annual meeting of the Southwestern Political Science Association, April 2–5, 1980.

Nabhan, Gary Paul. "Papago Fields: Arid Lands Ethnobotany and Agricultural Ecology." Ph.D. diss., University of Arizona, 1983.

Thomas, Robert K. "Papago Land Use West of the Papago Indian Reservation South of the Gila River and the Problem of Sand Papago Identity." Ithaca, New York, 1963. Mimeographed.

Tooker, Elisabeth J. "Papagos in Tucson: An Introduction to Their History, Community Life and Acculturation." University of Arizona Library, n.d. Mimeographed.


INTERVIEWS

Anton, Ascension. Interviewed by Floyd O'Neil and Winston Erickson. Interpreted by Anna Anton. Sept. 10, 1988.

Blaine, Peter. Interviewed by Floyd O'Neil and Bernard Siquieros. Sept. 11, 1988.

Daniel, Claudia. Interviewed by Bernard Siquieros, Floyd O'Neil, and June Lyman. Sept. 14, 1988.

Franco, Patrick Johnny. Interviewed by Floyd O'Neil and Bernard Siquieros. Sept. 9, 1988.

McCarty, James. Interviewed by Floyd O'Neil and Bernard Siquieros. Sept. 9, 1988.

Moore, Josiah. Several informal interviews by Winston Erickson and Floyd O'Neil.

Morris, Rufina. Interviewed by Floyd O'Neil and David Hoehner. Sept. 10, 1988.

Price, Clara Bonnie. Interviewed by Winston Erickson, David Hoehner, and June Lyman. Sept. 13, 1988.

Ramon, Lena. Interviewed by Floyd O'Neil and David Hoehner. Sept. 10, 1988.

Zunnie, Tulpo. Interviewed and translated by Rosilda Manuel. Sept. 13, 1988.

U.S. GOVERNMENT SOURCES

National Archives, Washington, D.C. Official Correspondence. RG75.

National Archives and Record Center, Laguna Nigel, Calif. Official Correspondence. RG75.

# Index

## About the Author

WINSTON P. ERICKSON received a B.A. in 1968 and an M.A. in 1976 in European history from the University of Utah.

Since 1981, Erickson has worked at the American West Center, a research branch of the University of Utah, where he developed curricular materials for the Ute Mountain Ute Tribe and assisted in a similar project for the Tohono O'odham.

Erickson has also researched traditional land-use patterns of the Ute Mountain Utes and of the Tesuque Pueblo in New Mexico, and has participated in collecting oral histories from members of several tribes.

Erickson participated in the establishment of archives for the Tohono O'odham Nation, the Ute Mountain Ute Tribe, and the pueblos of New Mexico, and he is working to establish an archive of the New Mexico pueblos' water use and rights.